AF593822

Keep this pocket-sized Frith book with you when you are visiting Thanet or on holiday.

Whether you are in your car or on foot, you will enjoy an evocative journey back in time. Compare the Thanet of old with what you can see today —see how the streets and bustling seafronts of its resort towns have changed and developed, how shops, hotels and other buildings have been altered or replaced; look at fine details such as lamp-posts, shop fascias and trade signs; and see the many alterations to the Thanet region that have taken place unnoticed during our lives, some of which we may have taken for granted.

At the turn of a page you will gain fascinating insights into Thanet's unique history.

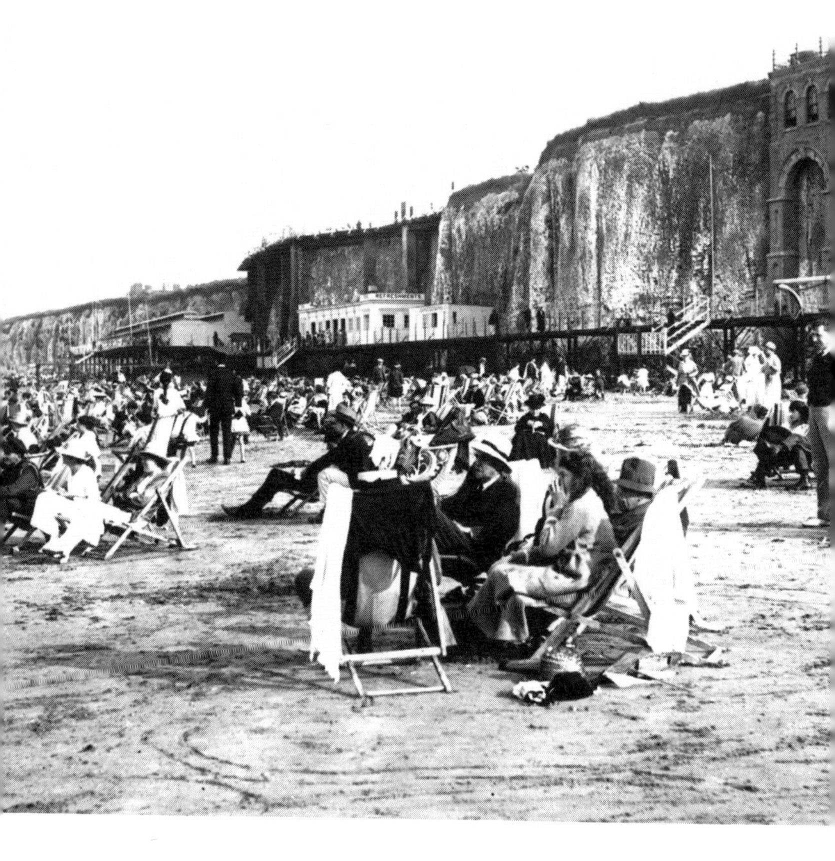

FRANCIS FRITH'S
pocket ALBUM

THANET

A POCKET ALBUM

Adapted from an original book by
HELEN LIVINGSTON

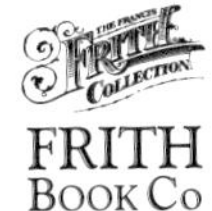

FRITH
BOOK CO

First published in the United Kingdom in 2003 by
Frith Book Company Ltd

ISBN 1-85937-718-1
Text and Design copyright © Frith Book Company Ltd
Photographs copyright © The Francis Frith Collection

The Frith photographs and the Frith logo are reproduced under licence from Heritage Photographic Resources Ltd, the owners of the Frith archive and trademarks

All rights reserved. No photograph in this publication may be sold to a third party other than in the original form of this publication, or framed for sale to a third party. No parts of this publication may be reproduced, stored in a retrieval system, or transmitted, in any form, or by any means, electronic, mechanical, photocopying, recording or otherwise, without the prior permission of the publishers and copyright holder.

British Library Cataloguing in Publication Data

Thanet—A Pocket Album
Adapted from an original book by Helen Livingston

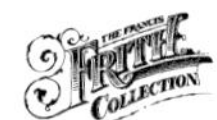

Frith Book Company Ltd
Frith's Barn, Teffont,
Salisbury, Wiltshire SP3 5QP
Tel: +44 (0) 1722 716 376
Email: info@francisfrith.co.uk
www.francisfrith.co.uk

Printed and bound in Great Britain by MPG, Bodmin

Front Cover: Margate Donkeys on the Sands 1906 / 54759 *The hand-colouring is for illustrative purposes only, and is not intended to be historically accurate.*

AS WITH ANY HISTORICAL DATABASE THE FRITH ARCHIVE IS CONSTANTLY BEING CORRECTED AND IMPROVED AND THE PUBLISHERS WOULD WELCOME INFORMATION ON OMISSIONS OR INACCURACIES

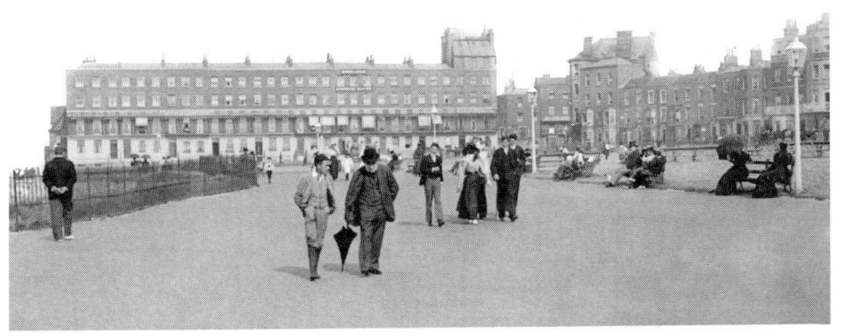

CONTENTS

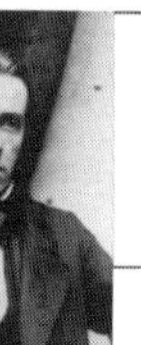

FRANCIS FRITH

VICTORIAN PIONEER

Francis Frith, founder of the world-famous photographic archive, was a complex and multi-talented man. A devout Quaker and a highly successful Victorian businessman, he was philosophic by nature and pioneering in outlook. By 1855 he had already established a wholesale grocery business in Liverpool, and sold it for the astonishing sum of £200,000, which is the equivalent today of over £15,000,000. Now in his thirties, and captivated by the new science of photography, Frith set out on a series of pioneering journeys up the Nile and to the Near East.

INTRIGUE AND EXPLORATION

He was the first photographer to venture beyond the sixth cataract of the Nile. Africa was still the mysterious 'Dark Continent', and Stanley and Livingstone's historic meeting was a decade into the future. The conditions for picture taking confound belief. He laboured for hours in his wicker dark-room in the sweltering heat of the desert, while the volatile chemicals fizzed dangerously in their trays. Back in London he exhibited his photographs and was 'rapturously cheered' by members of the Royal Society. His reputation as a photographer was made overnight.

VENTURE OF A LIFE-TIME

By the 1870s the railways had threaded their way across the country, and Bank Holidays and half-day Saturdays had been made obligatory by Act of Parliament. All of a sudden the working man and his family were able to enjoy days out, take holidays, and see a little more of the world.

With typical business acumen, Francis Frith foresaw that these new tourists would enjoy having souvenirs to commemorate their days out. For the next thirty years he travelled the country by train and by pony and trap, producing fine photographs of seaside resorts and beauty spots that were keenly bought by millions of Victorians. These prints were painstakingly pasted into family albums and pored over during the dark nights of winter, rekindling precious memories of summer excursions. Frith's studio was soon supplying retail shops all over the country, and by 1890 F Frith & Co had become the greatest specialist photographic publishing company in the world, with over 2,000 sales outlets, and pioneered the picture postcard.

FRANCIS FRITH'S LEGACY

Francis Frith had died in 1898 at his villa in Cannes, his great project still growing. The archive he created continued in business for another seventy years. By 1970 it contained over a third of a million pictures showing 7,000 British towns and villages.

Frith's legacy to us today is of immense significance and value, for the magnificent archive of evocative photographs he created provides a unique record of change in the cities, towns and villages throughout Britain over a century and more. Frith and his fellow studio photographers revisited locations many times down the years to update their views, compiling for us an enthralling and colourful pageant of British life and character.

We are fortunate that Frith was dedicated to recording the minutiae of everyday life. For it is this sheer wealth of visual data, the painstaking chronicle of changes in dress, transport, street layouts, buildings, housing, engineering and landscape that captivates us so much today, offering us a powerful link with the past and with the lives of our ancestors.

Computers have now made it possible for Frith's many thousands of images to be accessed almost instantly. The archive offers every one of us an opportunity to examine the places where we and our families have lived and worked down the years. Its images, depicting our shared past, are now bringing pleasure and enlightenment to millions around the world a century and more after his death.

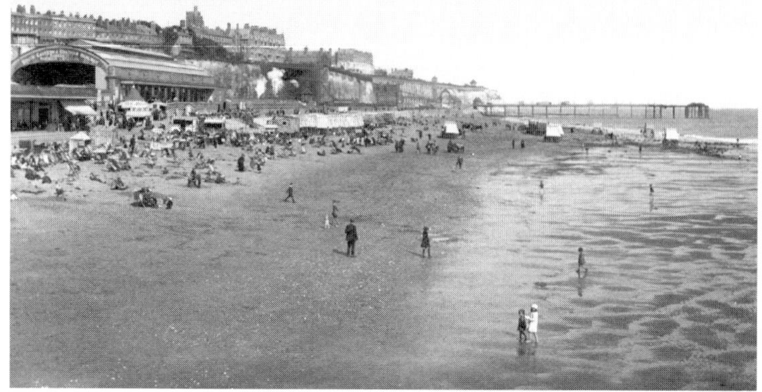

RAMSGATE, THE BEACH 1918 / 68460

THANET

AN INTRODUCTION

THIS STRETCH of coast in north-east Kent, from Margate round past the cliffs of the North Foreland with its famous lighthouse, and through Broadstairs to Ramsgate and Pegwell Bay, has been famed as Kent's leisure coast for well over a century. Replete with chalk cliffs, plenty of firm sandy bays, wide breezy promenades, Victorian hotels, interesting harbours and the whole gamut of seaside entertainments, it is not in the least surprising that holidaymakers have flocked here since the idea of the seaside holiday first took root.

The casual observer might be forgiven for dismissing the area as a string of resorts threaded along the cliffs and feeling down into the bays, and ranging from the decidedly 'honky-tonk' front at 'Merry Margate', through 'Riotous Ramsgate' with its yacht marina and modern harbour, to more select Broadstairs, still fondly dwelling on its memories of Charles Dickens. Yet this is only the surface. Beneath the modern cheeky image is a coast of great antiquity, the northern and eastern rim of the Isle of Thanet. Thanet was in truth an offshore island until the 14th century, but is now joined to the rest of Kent across an expanse of fertile farmland reclaimed from the sea. Even so, to reach the Isle of Thanet today you still have to cross a bridge over either the Wantsum or the River Stour.

The Isle of Thanet still possesses a strong sense of identity. At the time of the Romans it was separated from mainland Britain by the Wantsum Channel, a tidal inlet lying along the island's southern and western shores. Then, as now, Thanet's northern and eastern coasts—on which stand present-day Margate and Ramsgate—faced the North Sea and the English Channel. The Romans built forts on an island at Richborough (near Sandwich) and at Reculver (on the mainland) to guard the southern and northern mouths of the Wantsum. Until recently the historical significance of Richborough (Rutupiae) soared above that of any other place in Britain, for conventional history claims it to be the site of the successful Roman landing in AD43 under the Emperor Claudius. Although this view has been challenged by those who now argue that Fishbourne (near Chichester in Sussex) is a more likely spot for the landing of most of the 40,000-strong armed expeditionary force, there is little doubt of the importance of this corner of Kent to the Romans. Certainly Ramsgate (which some would, mistakenly, translate as 'Romansgate'—'where Caesar landed'), Broadstairs and probably Margate were inhabited in Roman times, and Roman remains have been found. In all likelihood they were Roman fishing villages with little harbours, but they probably also played a defensive role, especially in later Roman times.

Following the collapse of Roman rule in Britain, the Jutes and Saxons invaded Thanet's shores. Hengist and Horsa landed in Pegwell Bay at the southern end of the Wantsum Channel in 449

AD, and by 457 AD Hengist was able to proclaim himself King of Kent. Not quite a century and a half after this—in 597 AD—another 'invasion' took place at the same spot, when St Augustine and forty monks landed to preach Christianity to the English. A monastery was founded at Minster in 670 AD. In early Norman times a number of important churches were built in the Thanet villages that lay just inland from the sea coast - St John's (Margate) was founded in 1050, St Lawrence (Ramsgate) in 1062 and St Peter's (Broadstairs) in 1070. It is interesting that the silting up of the Wantsum Channel was in part deliberate, caused by highly successful drainage and reclamation works overseen initially by the monastic houses. By the 15th century the Wantsum Channel existed only in name, and the erstwhile port

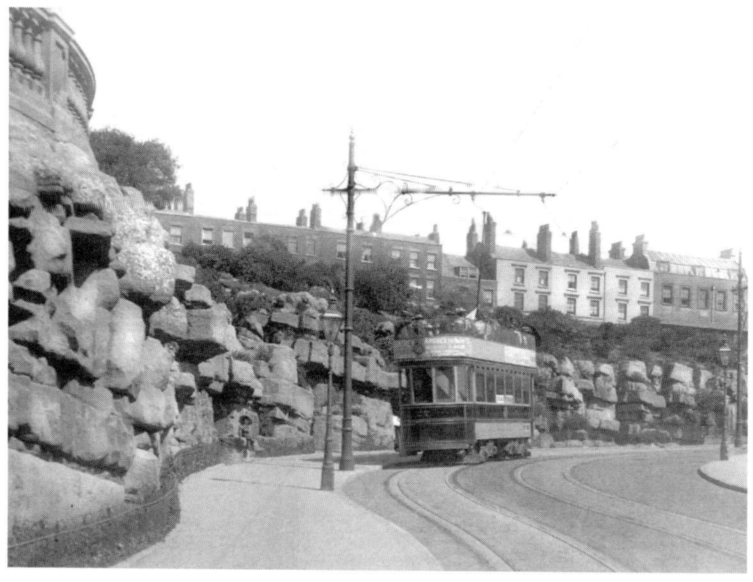

RAMSGATE, MADEIRA WALK 1901 / 48042

and ferry point of Minster-in-Thanet was forced to close. Even the great Cinque Port, Sandwich itself, at the southern end of the Wantsum channel, where the River Stour now flows out to sea, was suffering greatly from silting, a fact which allowed the development of Ramsgate as a port—it became a 'limb' of Sandwich in 1481. Indeed, Thanet's proximity to the continent meant that the jurisdiction of the Cinque Ports was always strong there. Margate was attached to Dover, and the Lord Warden of the Cinque Ports 'ordered' the choice of the pier wardens to collect the 'droits'.

Given its location, it is hardly surprising that there is a long history of seafaring in Thanet, including fishing in the waters off Iceland as well as the coastal trade and trade with Russia and the Baltic states. The many 'gates' along the coast—Westgate, Margate, Kingsgate, Ramsgate—were the gaps through the chalk cliffs whereby the sailormen reached the seashore.

The North Foreland lighthouse, built in the 17th century, warns shipping of the rocky Thanet coast against which many a ship has been wrecked. Offshore is the infamous shoal, the Goodwin Sands, swallower of countless ships; Thanet's maritime tradition is most nobly recorded in the service of its lifeboatmen.

The little harbours at Margate, Broadstairs and Ramsgate were in truth the very pulse of small seafaring communities, waxing strong in times of good harvest and drying to a small trickle when the spectre of famine arose. In time, as ships grew in size, the trade at the small harbours diminished, with the notable exception of the harbour at Ramsgate; today it is an important cross-channel ferry port which also trades with the Baltic.

Ramsgate harbour was constructed in 1749-91 following a disastrous storm. Its main architect was John Smeaton. The outer harbour—approved by Parliament in 1749—was created as a 'harbour of refuge' to provide a safe haven for shipping in bad weather. Smeaton constructed a dry dock here in 1791, which was in use for some 80 years before being converted to an ice store for the fishing fleet. It was restored in the 1980s. In 1821 George IV used Ramsgate as his point of embarkation in his journey to Hanover, and on his return decreed that Ramsgate harbour be a 'Royal Harbour'. An obelisk commemorates this. During the 1880s Ramsgate had the largest fishing fleet in south-east England—144 vessels all told. The fishing fleet moved to Brixham in Devon in the mid 20th century. Margate and Broadstairs also have their little harbours, protected by stone piers. The destruction of Broadstairs' pier in 1767 spelt disaster to the fisherfolk engaged in the Iceland cod fisheries. A new pier was built in 1808.

The present resorts of Margate, Broadstairs and Ramsgate grew from the pre-existing fishing villages, and were established in the early years of the 18th century. Like many other seaside watering places—Scarborough and Brighton, for example—they really started to grow following the publication in 1750 of Dr Richard Russell's famous treatise on the use of sea water for treatment of 'diseases of the glands'. Russell was a Sussex doctor; convinced that drinking and/or bathing in sea water was a powerful curative for a range of ailments, he advised his patients to visit the coast. His work was so influential that the fashionable world forsook the inland spas, such as Bath, Tunbridge Wells and Epsom, and headed for the coast. The new coastal resorts mimicked the old inland spas, and set out to provide all the social and fashionable conventions required by the visitors. Dances and other entertainments were presided over by a Master of Ceremonies, and the resorts themselves were equipped with a parade (usually 'fronting' the sea or along the pier), an assembly room, a theatre, a circulating library and a band.

Margate, Broadstairs and Ramsgate, on the cliffed Thanet coast with its small sandy bays, were conveniently close to London, and indeed might have been tailor-made to fit Dr Russell's prescription of the ideal coastal resort: '... one would choose the shore to be sandy and flat, for the convenience of going down into the sea in a bathing chariot ... that the sea shore should be bounded by lively cliffs, and downs; to add to the chearfulness of the place, and give the person that has bathed an opportunity of mounting on horseback dry and clean; to pursue such exercises, as may be advised by his physician, after he comes out of the bath ...' The 'bathing chariots' mentioned in this extract were none other than bathing machines, in effect horse-drawn changing rooms, in which bathers could be carried out into the shallow coastal waters. They are reputedly the invention of a Margate Quaker, Benjamin Beale, though the Yorkshire resort of Scarborough disputes Margate's claim to the

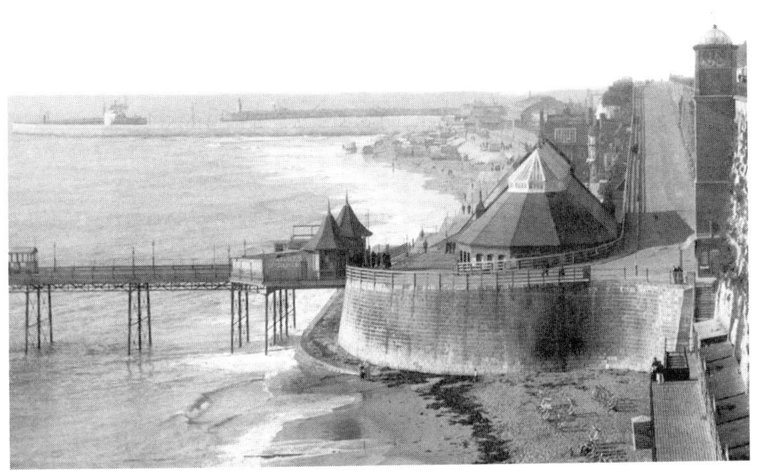

RAMSGATE, VIEW FROM EAST CLIFF 1918 / 68464

invention, and it has been suggested that Beale only added the canvas covers which increased the 'gentility' of the contraptions by allowing the bather to enter and leave the water unobserved.

Margate's Royal Sea-Bathing Infirmary, opened in 1796, was the first of its kind in the world. Here poor patients were able to take a sea-water cure. As late as 1856 it was connected with the Radcliffe Infirmary at Oxford. Where Margate led, other resorts followed suit, since the Thanet coast was celebrated for its salubrious air, and infirmaries and convalescent homes proliferated. Broadstairs was particularly favoured, and many an invalid travelled there to recuperate. Further along the coast, Pegwell was known for its Working Men's Convalescent Home which is pictured later in the book.

Considering its present reputation for seaside fun, it is perhaps only right to add that Margate also lays claim to be the first resort to

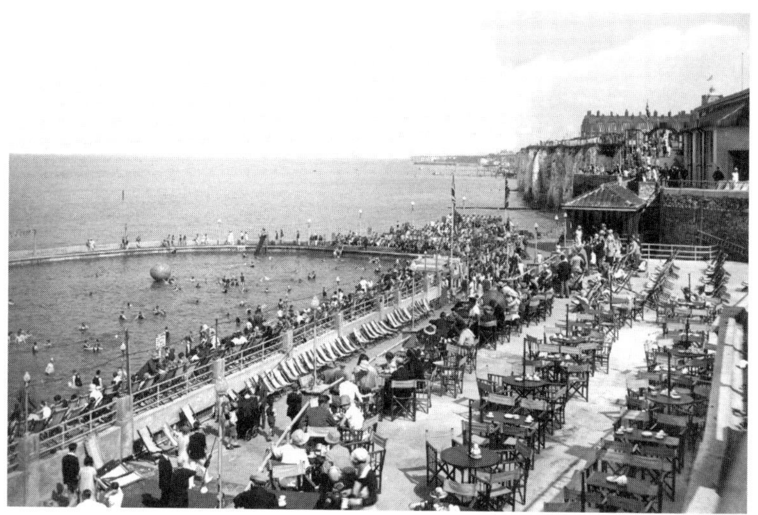

MARGATE, CLIFTONVILLE BATHING POOL *1927 / 80348*

use donkey-rides as an amusement—particularly, it seems, for the ladies. From about 1800 a Mr Bennett, who lived in the High Street, kept donkeys for hire at one shilling an hour.

Thanet's proximity to London was important, and Margate was the first ever popular resort; it drew London crowds by boat long before the railways carried them to such places as Brighton. The old Margate 'hoys', flat-bottomed cargo boats, made for an uncomfortable but relatively cheap journey, which would normally take about 10-14 hours—but up to three days if wind and tides were unfavourable. A 1789 Margate Guide suggested that few people 'in genteel life' would travel by hoy 'unless recommended by their physicians to do so, in order to experience sea sickness, which is thought to be very beneficial in some cases'! Many preferred to travel by stage coach or private chaise, despite the fact that the unsurfaced Thanet roads left much to be desired. In about 1815 steamboats began to replace the hoys, but it was the coming of the railway in 1846 (South Eastern Railway) and 1863 (London, Chatham and Dover Railway) which led to the thorough development of Thanet as Kent's leisure coast.

The accessibility of the coastal resorts of Thanet was increased by the arrival of the Isle of Thanet Electric Tramways and Lighting Company, which commenced its tram service in 1901, following on from a horse-drawn tram system. The Thanet trams were a short-lived phenomenon and fell victim to the bus service after the First World War. Today, road travel by car or coach is the most popular way to travel around the area.

During the First World War the Thanet resorts suffered from bombing and shelling. Civilian lives were lost, and property damaged and destroyed. Thanet faced across the sea to the battlefields of Europe; a seaplane base was constructed at Westgate in 1914—planned before hostilities commenced—and a Royal Naval Air

Service airfield opened at Manston in 1915. Ramsgate in particular was badly affected, with much damage caused by 'dump raids', particularly in 1917. On 31 October that year the gasworks were bombed. Despite this, the Thanet resorts remained open throughout the war; among these pictures are some remarkable seaside scenes taken during the summer of 1918, in which there seems to be no spectre of the trenches such a short distance away. During the Second World War, however, Thanet was in the front line, and her beaches were prohibited areas. The Winter Gardens at Margate, open throughout the first conflict, were used as a receiving station for allied troops evacuated from Dunkirk, but the pavilion received a direct hit in 1941. There were gun emplacements along the cliffs and anti-invasion defences on Ramsgate Sands - after the war, tons of explosives had to be cleared from the beach. RAF Manston had the longest runway in the world, and accepted hundreds of bombers a day.

The pictures in this book concentrate on the resorts and harbours, and show delightfully that the Thanet coast has been given over to the seaside holiday from Victorian times onward. Here are pictures of Margate's jetty in its heyday. It was a much-loved pleasure pier, unfortunately lost in a storm in 1978. It was built between 1853 and 1855 on the site of Jarvis's Landing Place, a structure dating from 1824; it had allowed steamboats to dock at low tide when they could not reach the harbour pier. Also pictured here are Ramsgate's vanished Promenade Pier and the former pier at Pegwell.

The pictures have been arranged so as to present a tour of the coast from Westgate eastwards through Margate and Cliftonville to Kingsgate and the North Foreland; then through Broadstairs, Ramsgate and Pegwell Bay to Minster, overlooking the green fields that now cover the southern arm of that once-busy shipping lane, the Wantsum Channel.

WESTGATE ON SEA

GENERAL VIEW 1889 / 22302

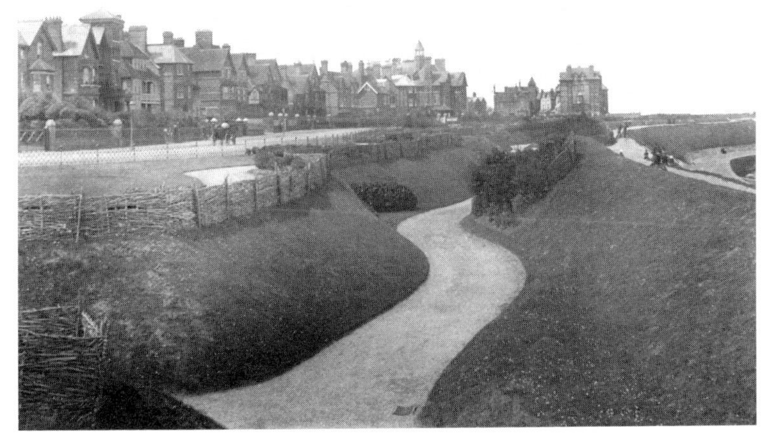

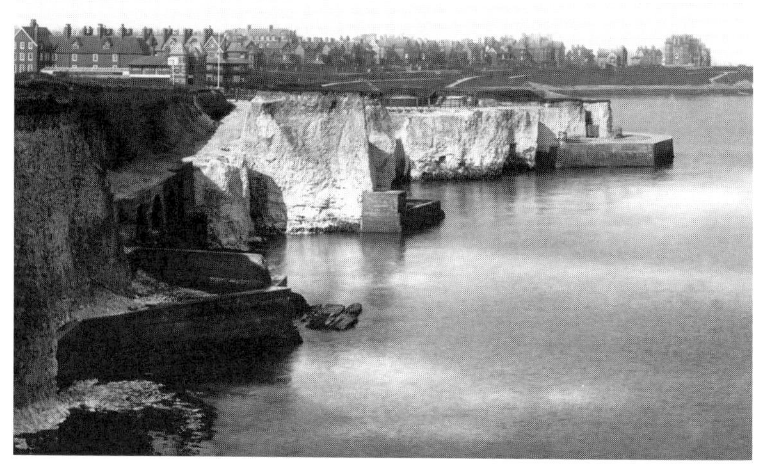

Westgate developed as a seaside resort during the 1870s—previously, there was only a farmhouse here. We are looking westwards to the Victorian skyline of Westgate and along the cliffs to Ledge Point. At the time this picture was taken, Tower House Retreat at Westgate, founded in 1879, was the only building in the United Kingdom built specifically for 'the treatment of intemperance'.

WESTGATE ON SEA

FROM THE CLIFFS 1892 / 31450

WESTGATE ON SEA

GENERAL VIEW 1890 / 27462

This fine view of St Mildred's Bay shows how little built up it was in the early 1890s. Note the two bathing machines on the left under the low chalk cliffs. Victorian ladies stroll on the promenade—note the lady pushing a pram in the centre—and holiday makers enjoy themselves on the beach.

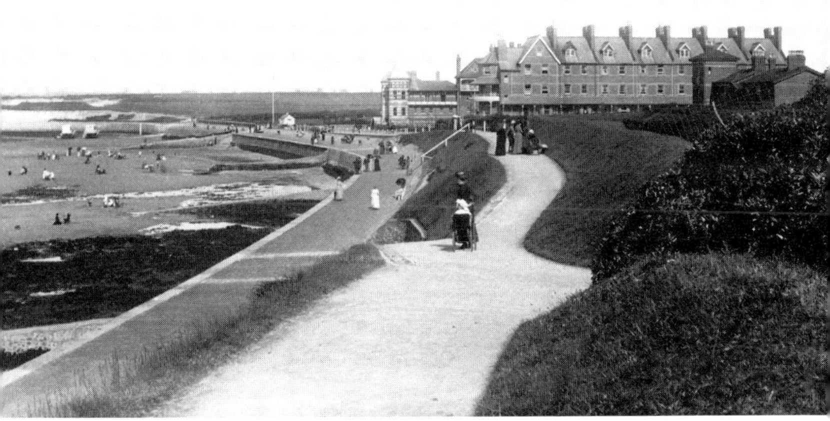

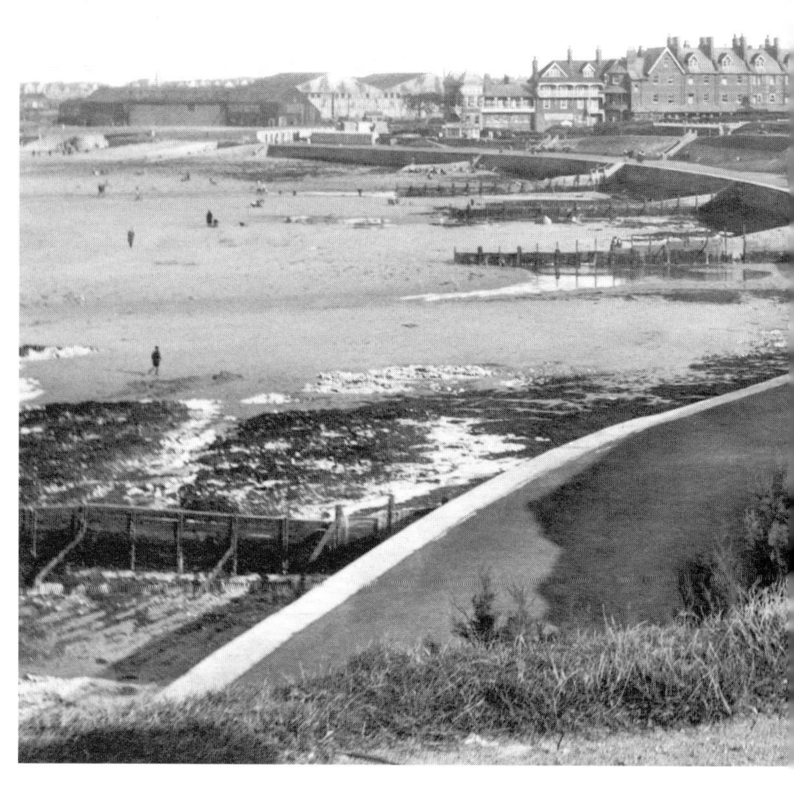

WESTGATE ON SEA

ST MILDRED'S BAY LOOKING EAST 1918 / 68422

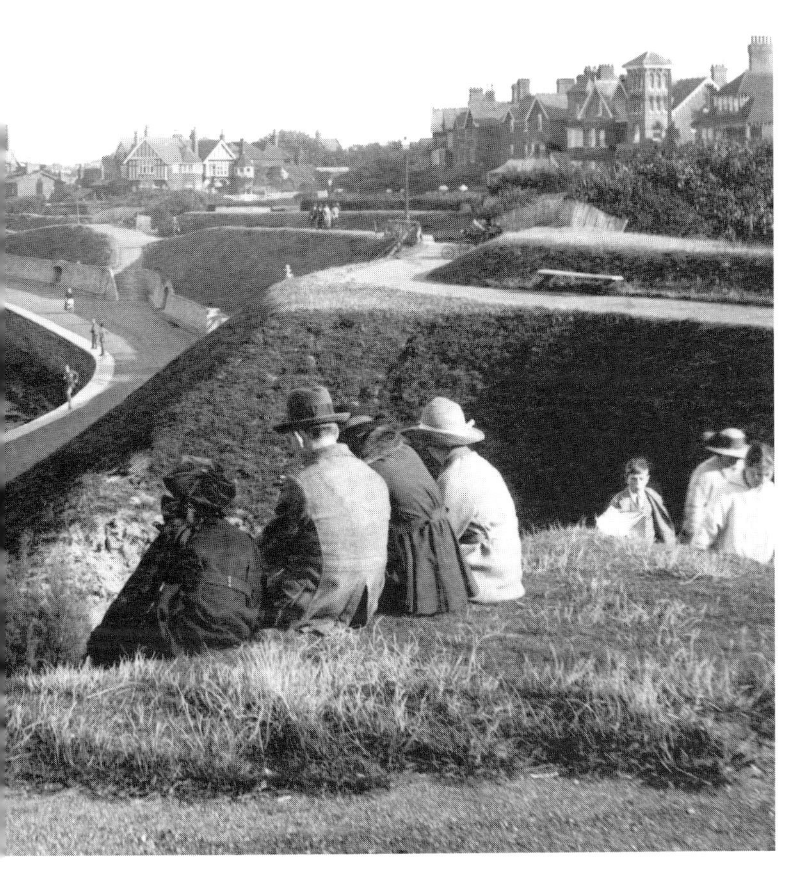

This is a similar view to photograph No 27462, but taken perhaps a generation later: the fashions speak of a new era. During the First World War, St Mildred's Bay was taken over as a Royal Naval Air Service Station, with a tented camp set up on the grassy promenade.

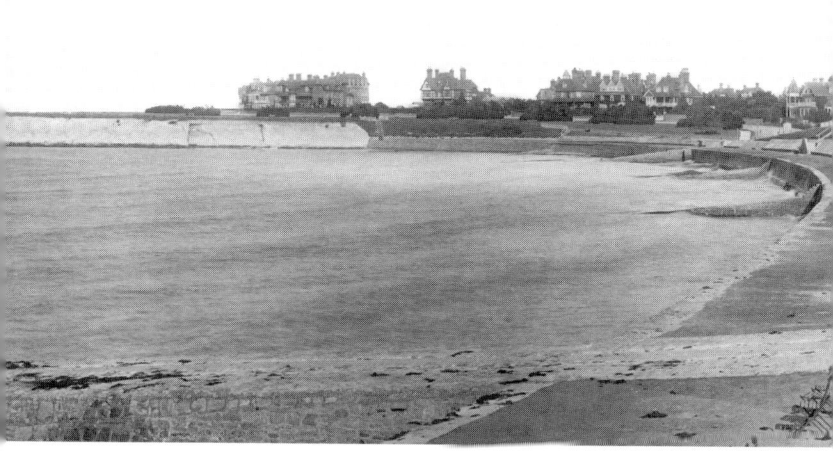

This view looks east around West Bay to Ledge Point, showing the neat, enclosed little bay and the lack of noisy entertainment that, even a century ago, set Westgate apart from its neighbour, 'merry Margate'.

WESTGATE ON SEA

WEST BAY 1899 / 44810

It is some twenty years on from photograph number 44810, and West Bay has changed little. Note the bathing tents on the promenade. Westgate is known for the firm sands of both its little bays.

WESTGATE ON SEA

WEST BAY 1918 / 68424

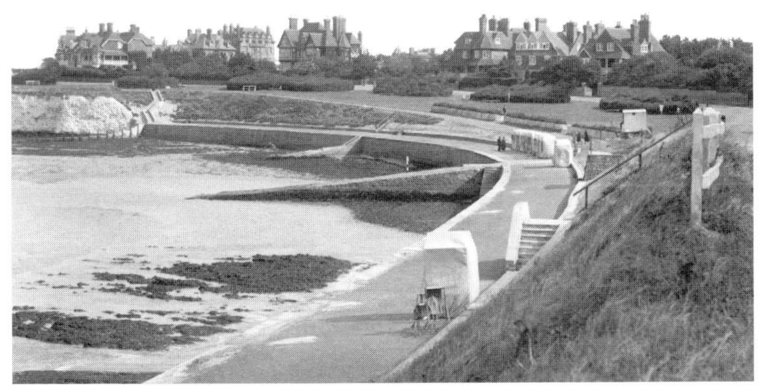

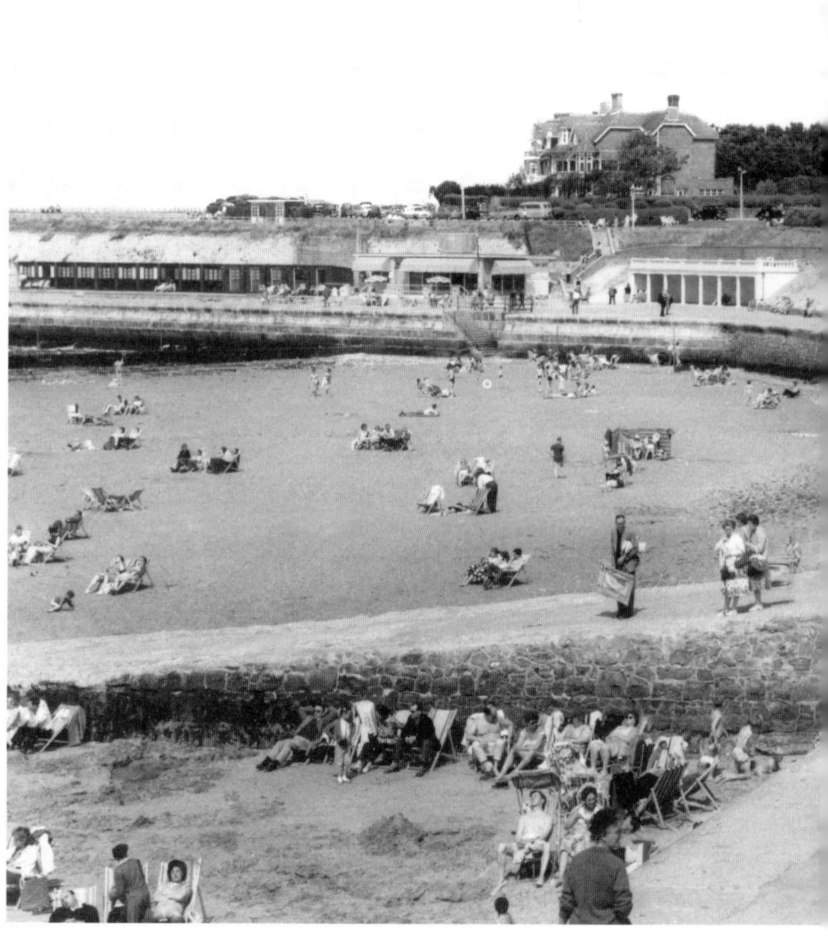

WESTGATE ON SEA

WEST BAY c1965 / W280026

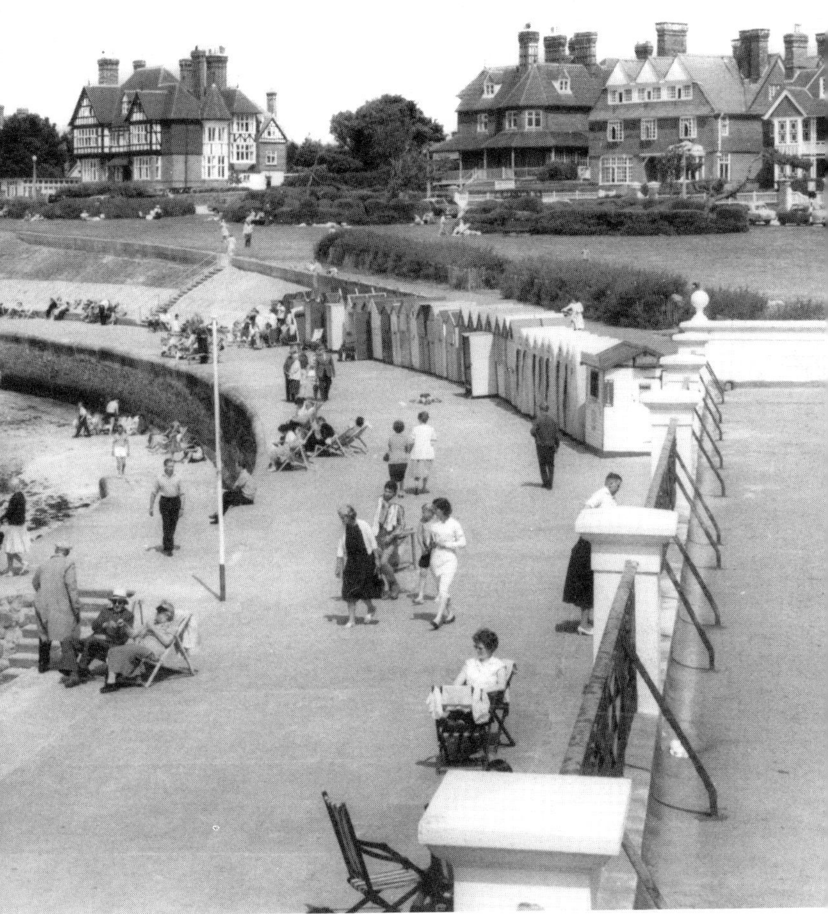

These are some of the substantial red brick houses built along the coast at Westgate in the prosperous late Victorian era—the 1880s and 90s. Note their gables and dormers, and their first floor balconies affording that envied view to the sea. These family homes are now all hotels of one sort or another.

WESTGATE ON SEA

SEA ROAD 1897 / 40172

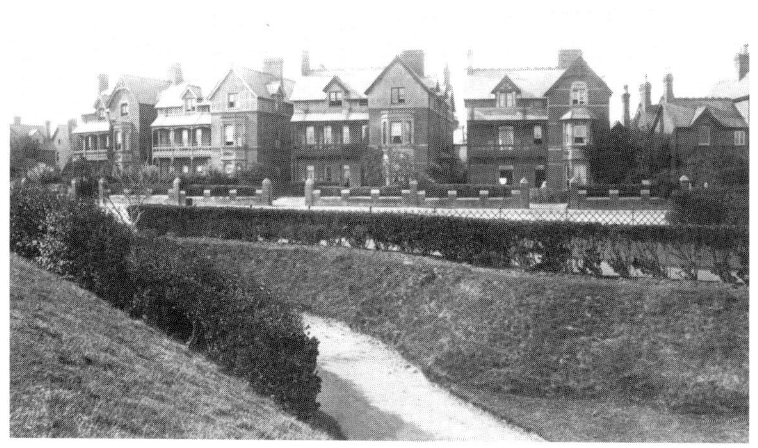

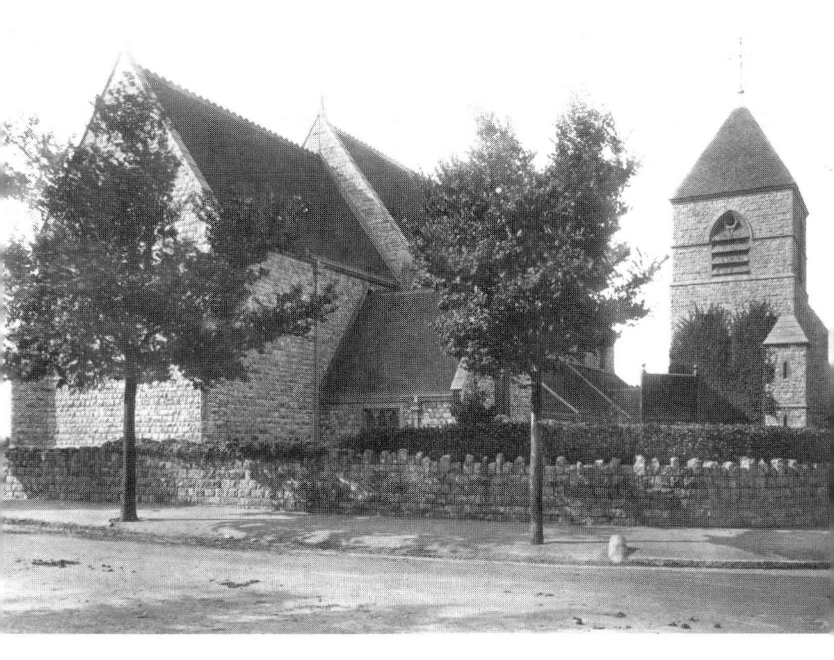

St Saviour's church was built in 1883-84 of Kentish rag. The foundation stone was laid in 1883 by Sir Erasmus Wilson, a famous surgeon, who popularised Westgate for its health-giving air. The church, by C N Beazley, is unusual in that its north tower is detached and acts as a porch.

WESTGATE ON SEA

THE CHURCH 1897 / 40174

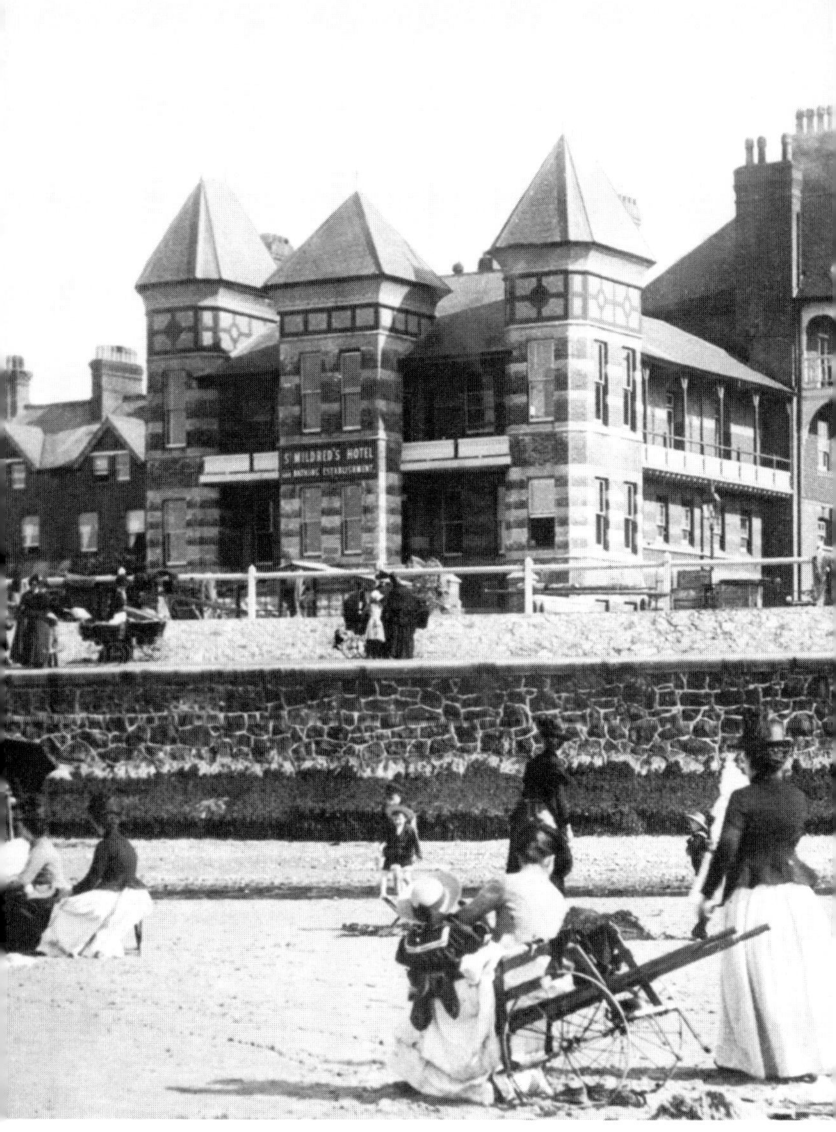

St MILDRED'S HOTEL

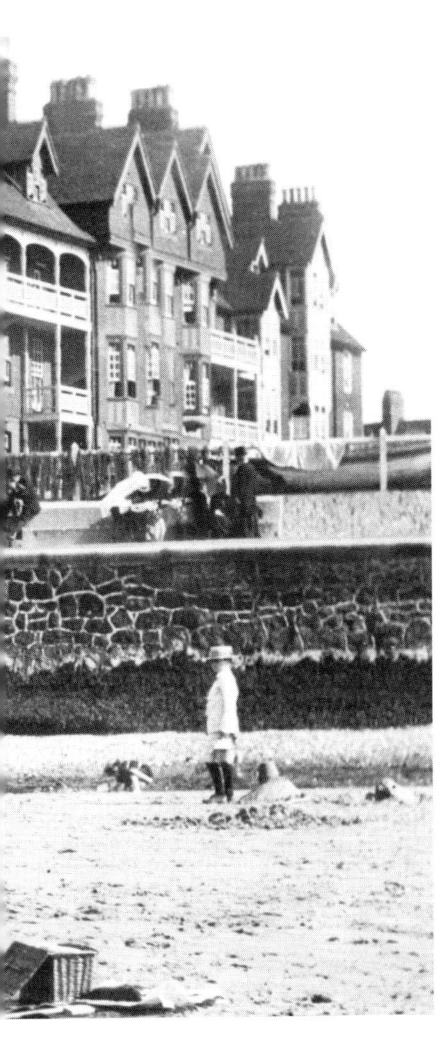

Here we see St Mildred's Hotel and the beach, with Victorian ladies and children at play. Note the picnic hamper on the right. Sir William Ingram, proprietor of St Mildred's Hotel, owned a large part of Westgate. During the First World War, St Mildred's Hotel became the headquarters of the seaplane base.

WESTGATE ON SEA

THE BEACH AND THE HOTELS
1890 / 27463

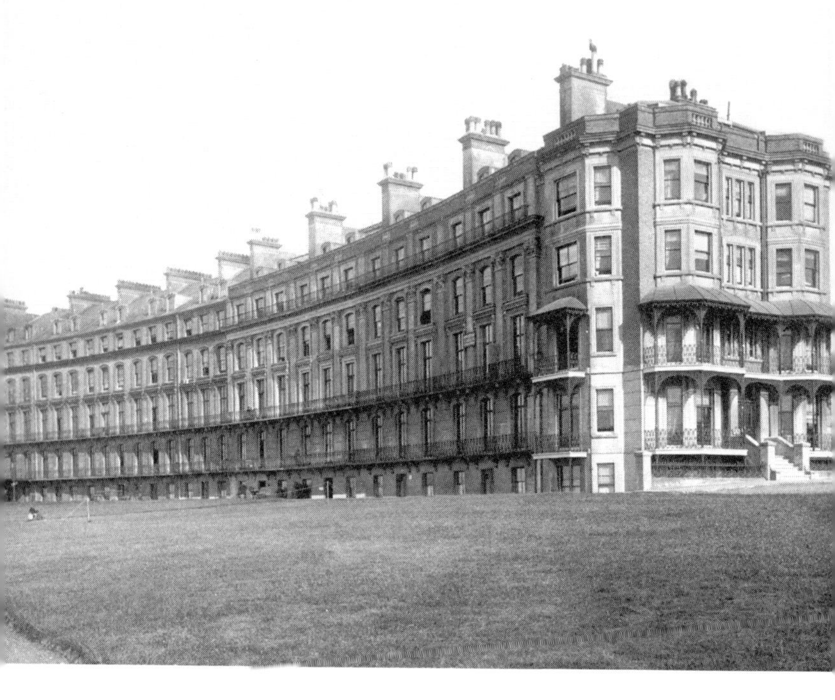

This superb picture shows the magnificent sweep of Nayland Crescent at the western end of town, close to the Royal Sea-Bathing Hospital and the infamous Nayland Rocks.

MARGATE

NAYLAND CRESCENT 1890 / 27443

Now occupied by the Winter Gardens, the Fort, also known as Fort Green, stood high up on the sea cliff east of Margate Harbour where a gun battery had stood during the Napoleonic wars. The area formed a recreation ground with a central bandstand. The houses of Fort Crescent, which run across this picture, were built in the 1820s—it was the most fashionable part of Margate at that time.

MARGATE

THE FORT 1887 / 19703

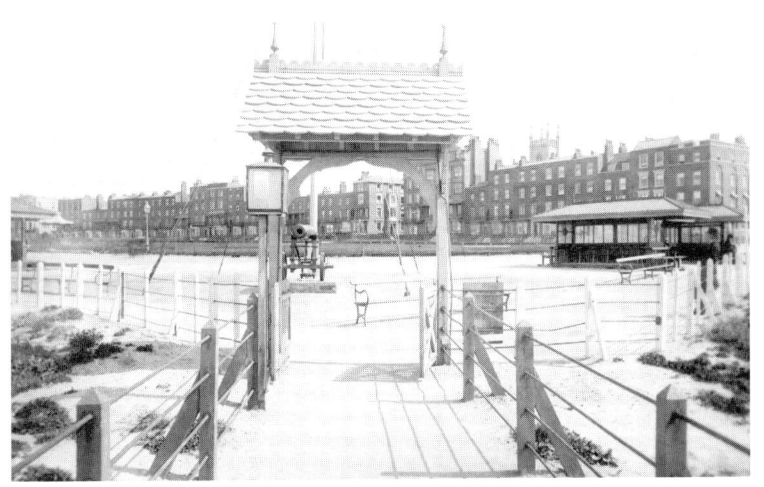

This splendid view of the site of the former cliff-top fort was taken prior to the extension of the cliff-foot promenade. The terrace of houses in the centre of the picture, Fort Paragon, was constructed soon after the Napoleonic Wars, certainly before 1830, as were the houses of Fort Crescent, on the right. The bandstand is late 19th-century.

MARGATE

THE FORT 1892 / 31441

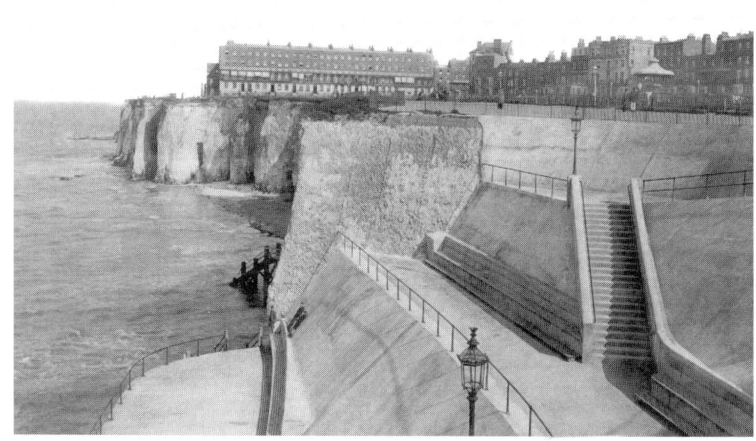

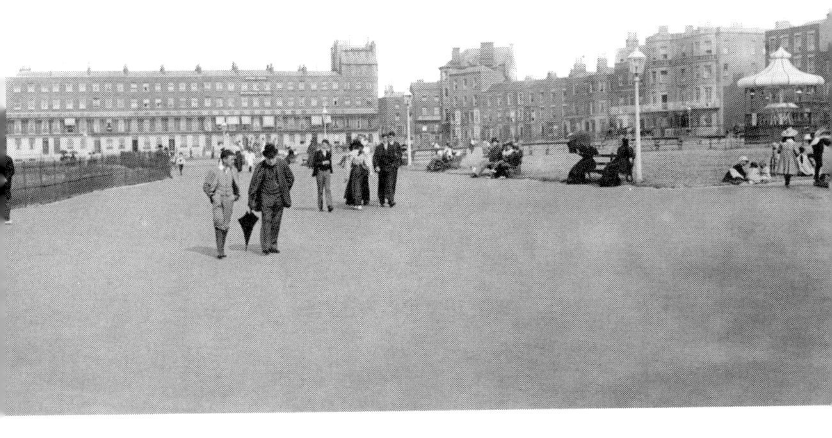

Late Victorian holiday-makers, taking the sea air, are strolling and sitting in the former recreation ground at Fort Green, looking towards Fort Paragon. The bandstand is on the right.

MARGATE

THE FORT 1897 / 39582

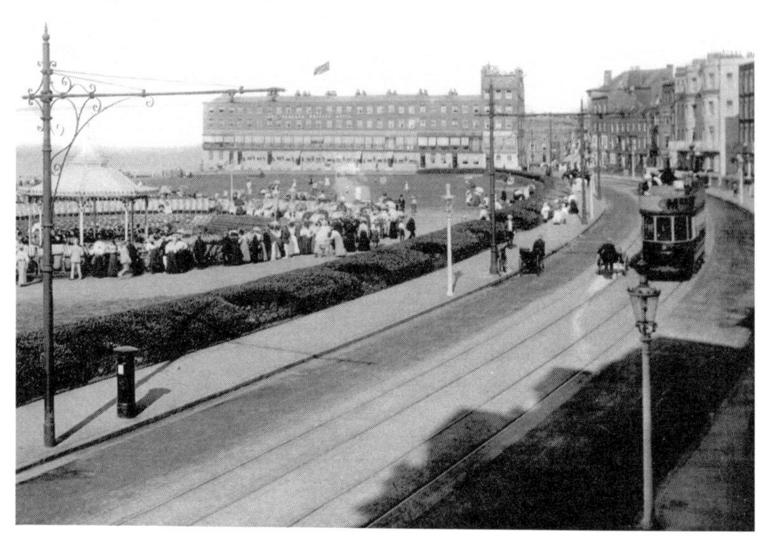

A concert is taking place at the bandstand at The Fort, a few seasons before massive construction work took place here to create the new Pavilion and Winter Gardens. The tram running along Fort Crescent has come from Cliftonville. The Isle of Thanet Electric Tramways and Lighting Company began its tram service in 1901.

MARGATE

THE BANDSTAND AND THE SEA FRONT 1908 / 60377

MARGATE

THE PAVILION AND THE WINTER GARDENS 1918 / 68439

The Pavilion and Winter Gardens on the site of The Fort were opened on 3 August 1911. Construction work had not begun until the previous November, with over 43,000 cubic yards of chalk excavated and used as infill for the new promenade. The Winter Gardens remained open during the First World War.

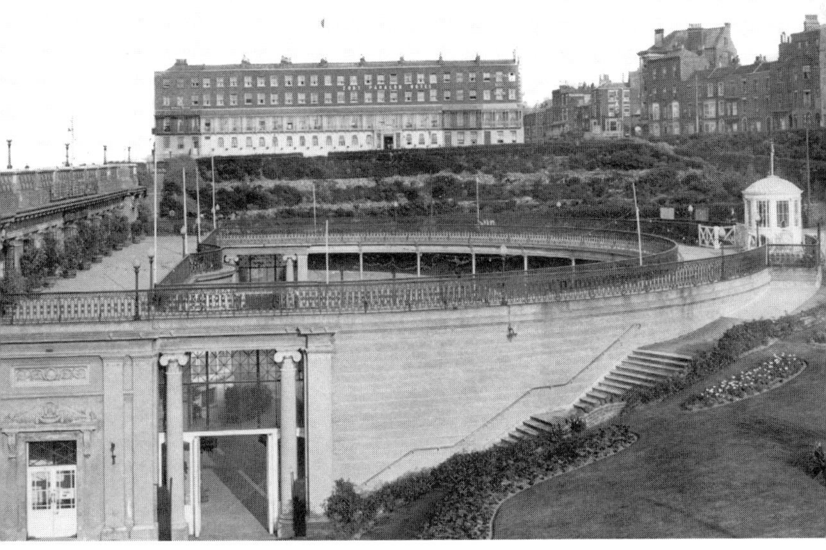

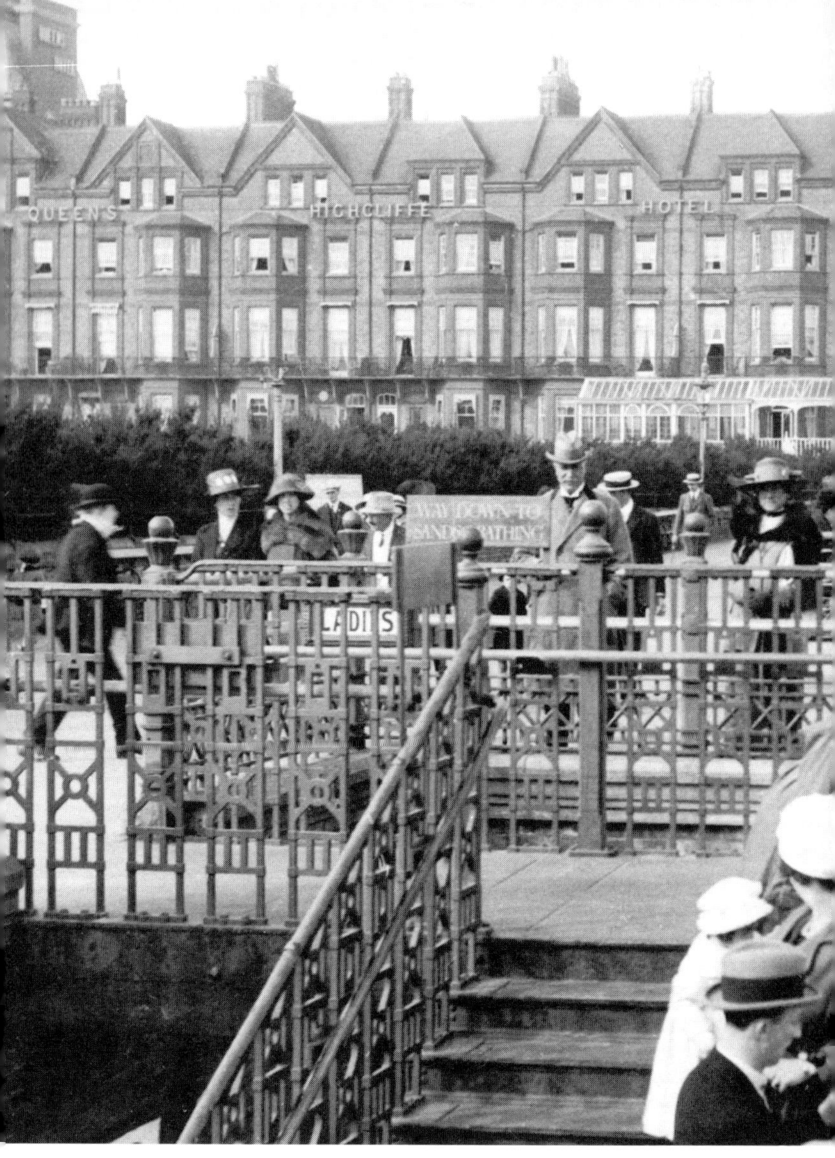
QUEEN'S
HIGHCLIFFE
HOTEL

MARGATE

THE PROMENADE AND THE CLIFFS 1918 / 68433

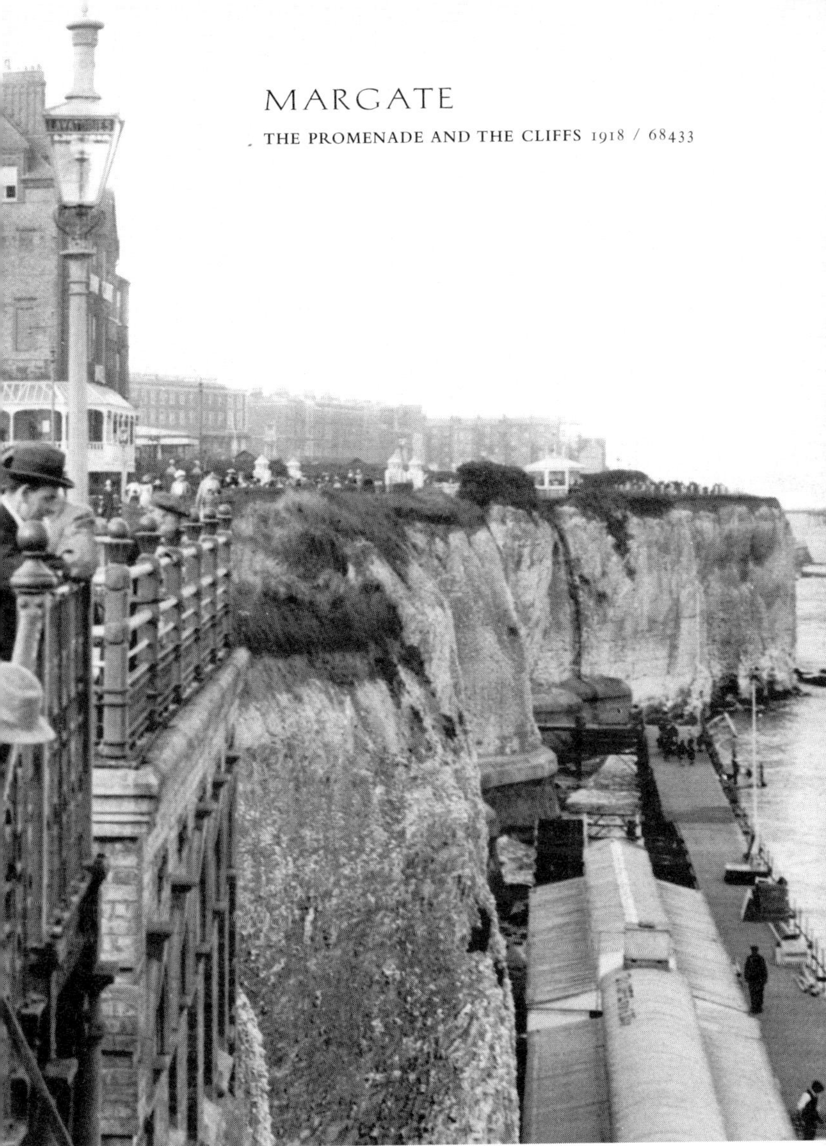

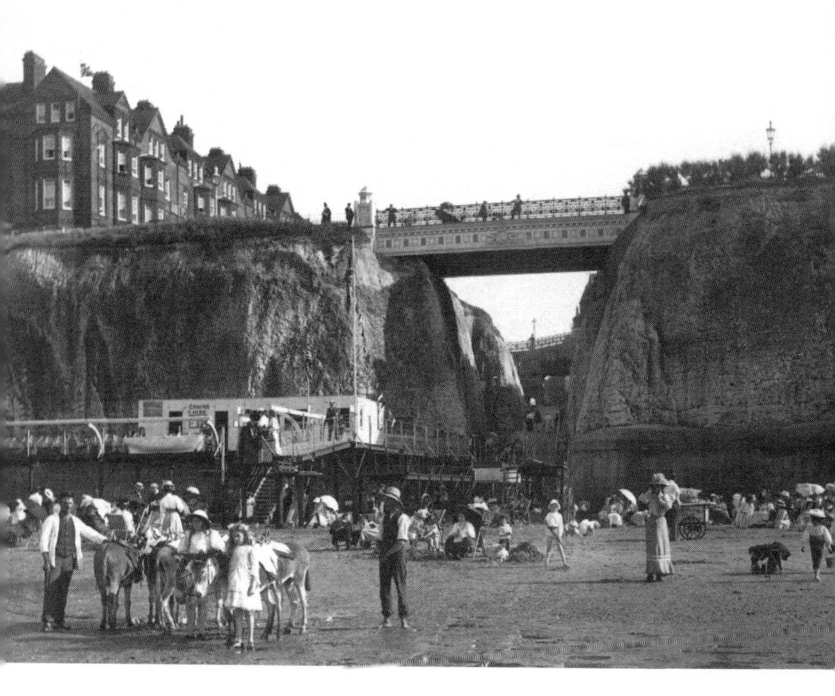

The present footbridge over Newgate Gap was built in 1907; it replaced the one constructed in 1861 by Captain Frederick Hodges. The new bridge shown in this picture was part of the fiftieth anniversary celebrations of Margate's incorporation as a borough.

MARGATE

NEWGATE GAP 1908 / 60373

We are looking east along Newgate promenade towards the Highcliffe Hotel (visible on the left), with groups of Victorian holidaymakers strolling in the sun. In the centre is the white façade of the Cliftonville Hotel, where now stand Thorley's public house and a bowling alley. The luxurious Cliftonville was built in 1868; it sported its own tennis courts, croquet lawns and cricket pitch. It was demolished in 1962.

MARGATE

THE PROMENADE 1897 / 39581

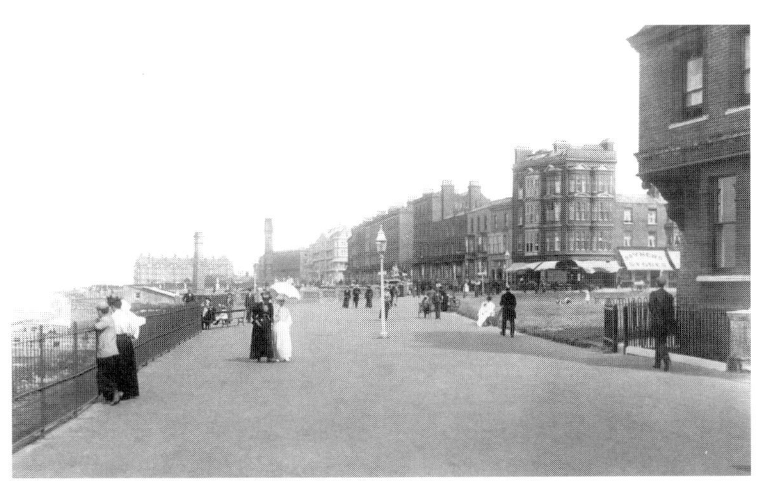

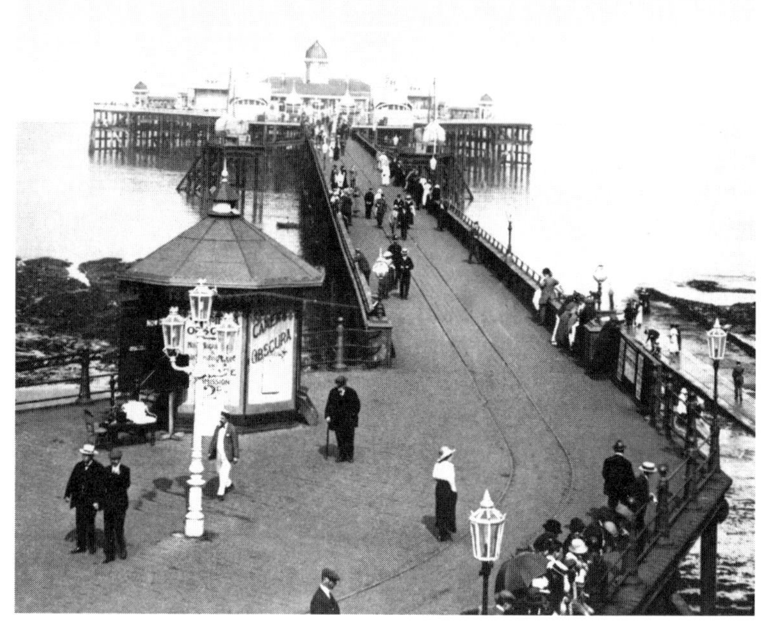

We are looking north along the jetty towards the hexagonal Jetty Extension of 1877. The extension, apart from its importance as a landing stage for steamers, also sported a restaurant and a bandstand. The small kiosk in the centre of the picture housed the camera obscura, which reflected a view of the surrounding area into a large white dish.

MARGATE

THE JETTY 1918 / 68444

MARGATE

THE JETTY FROM THE FORT 1897 / 39579

The Jetty at Margate was to all intents and purposes a pleasure pier. Always known as 'the Jetty' to distinguish it from the pre-existing harbour pier, it was 1,240 ft long. The Jetty was a popular attraction—it is very sad that it was destroyed by a storm in 1978.

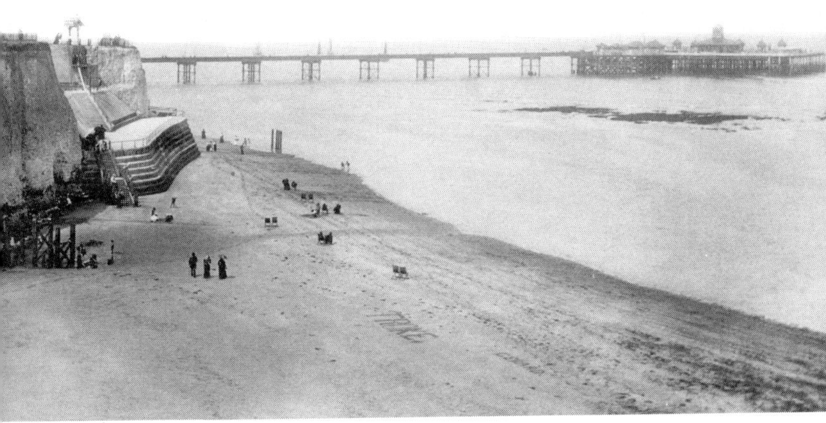

This crowded beach scene shows minstrels performing on the sands. In the eighties and nineties of the 19th century the most famous Margate 'negro', his face blackened by burnt cork, was 'Uncle Bones'—actually Alfred Bourne, a native of Margate. His legendary performances won him a huge following, and he has been described as 'a Margate institution'.

MARGATE

THE SANDS 1906 / 54756

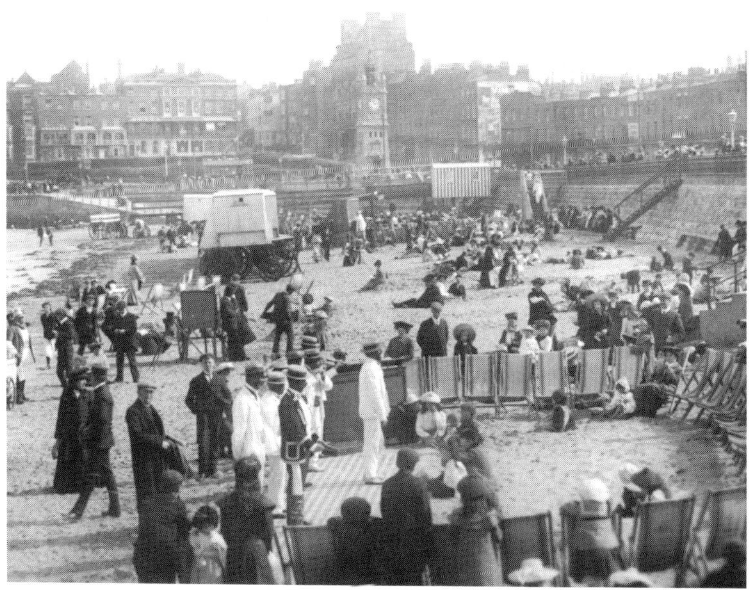

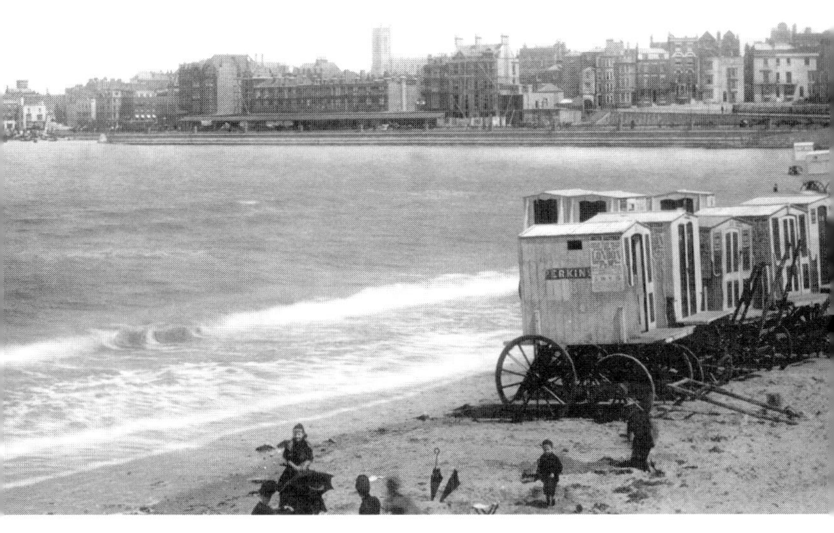

The development of Margate as a resort was founded on the craze for sea bathing. In this picture bathing machines owned by Edward Perkins line the beach. Mr Perkins, who described himself as 'bathing machine proprietor and furniture remover', also provided bathing costumes. The covered bathing machine was the invention of a Margate man, a Quaker called Benjamin Beale, who was born in about 1717.

MARGATE

THE BEACH AND THE BATHING MACHINES 1887 / 19869

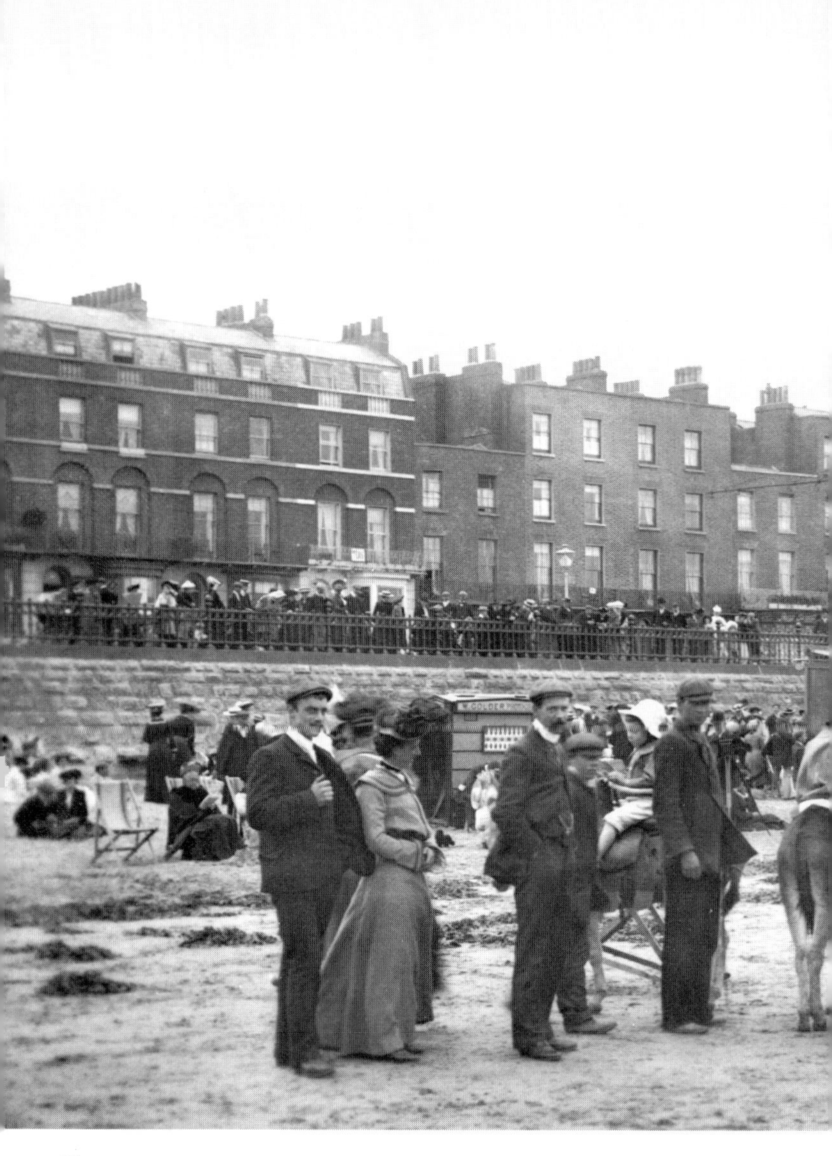

MARGATE

THE SANDS 1906 / 54758

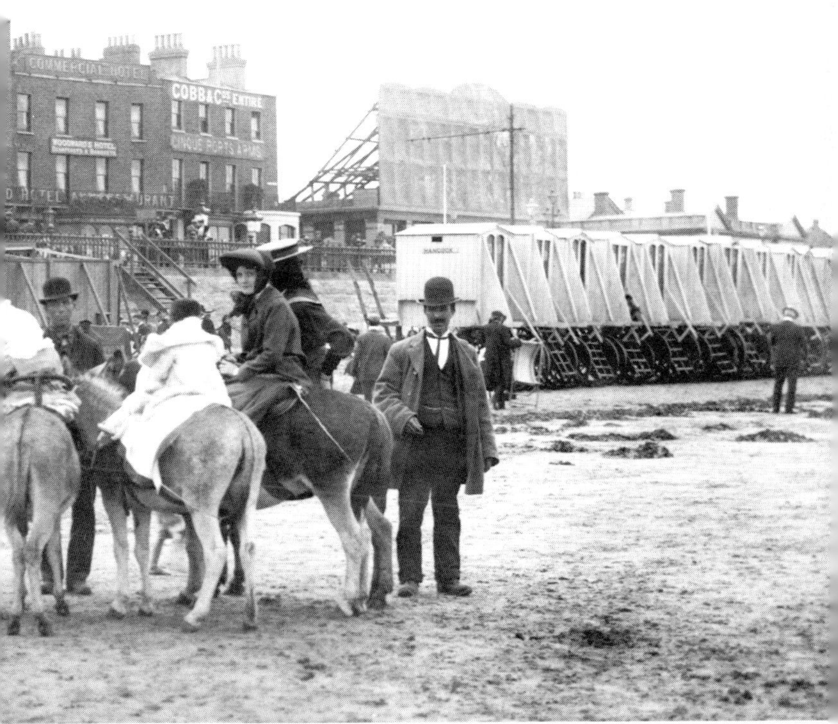

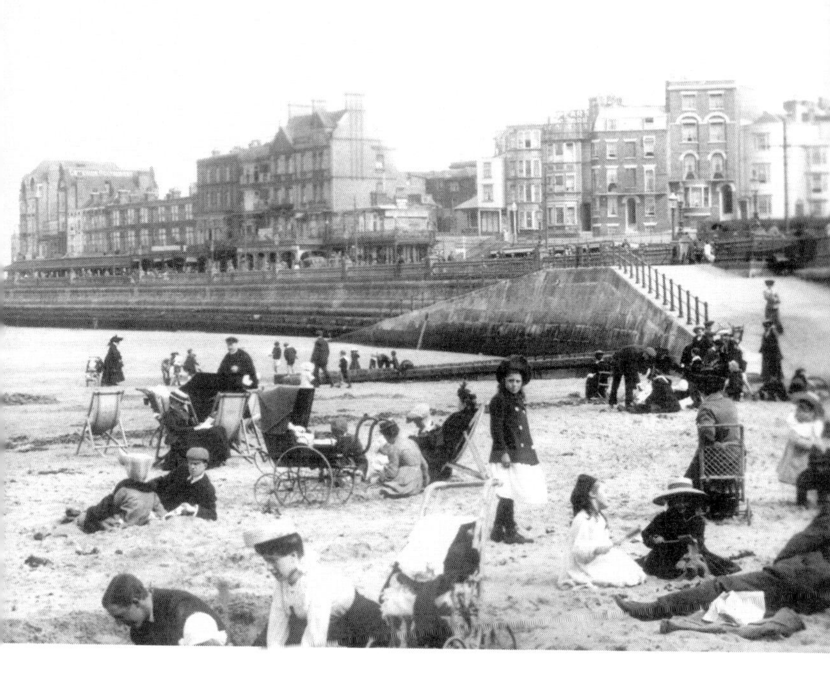

Holidaymakers enjoy themselves on Margate Beach. Note the prams in the centre of the picture, and that virtually everyone seems to be fully clothed and wearing a hat of some sort.

MARGATE

THE BEACH 1906 / 54757

A large crowd gathers around Edward Perkins' bathing platform on the gently sloping Margate Sands. Bathers were taken by this horse-drawn contrivance out to the water's edge and the bathing machines and diving boards. On the beach sandcastles are built, and happy families enjoy the carefree atmosphere.

MARGATE

THE SANDS 1906 / 54760

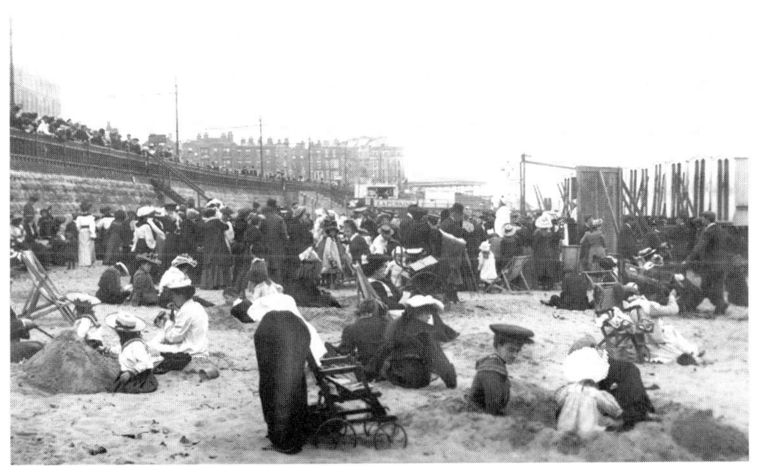

This view of the donkeys and their handlers, the 'donkey boys', also includes, on the right, the portable darkroom used by Frith's photographer. Behind is a row of bathing machines.

MARGATE

DONKEYS ON THE SANDS 1906 / 54759

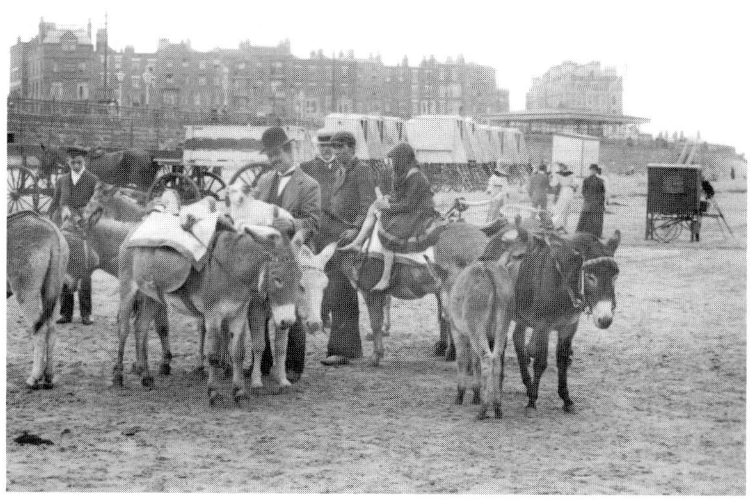

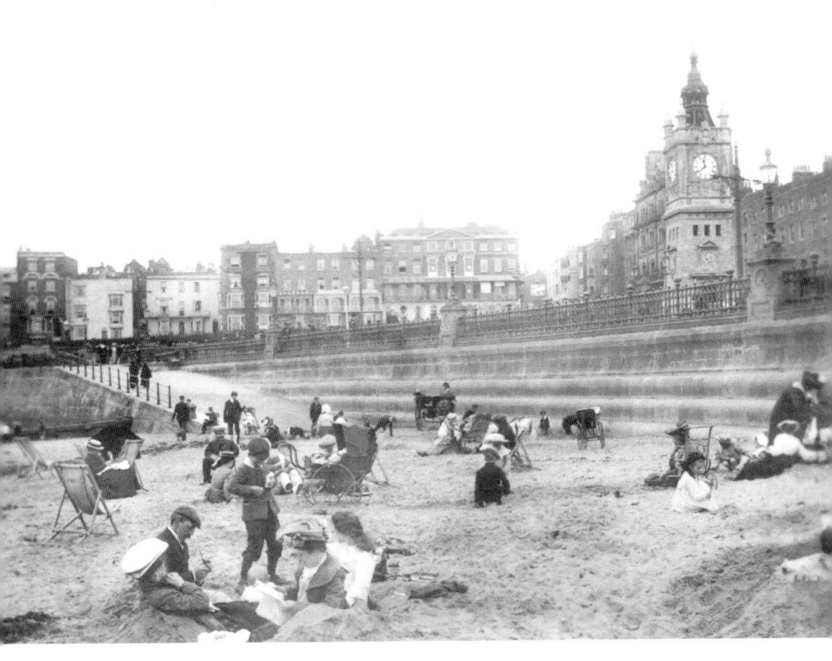

Margate's famous Jubilee clock tower is prominent in this picture of the beach. The 70 ft high tower was erected to commemorate Queen Victoria's Golden Jubilee in 1887, and was formally handed over to the corporation in 1889.

MARGATE

THE BEACH 1906 / 54761

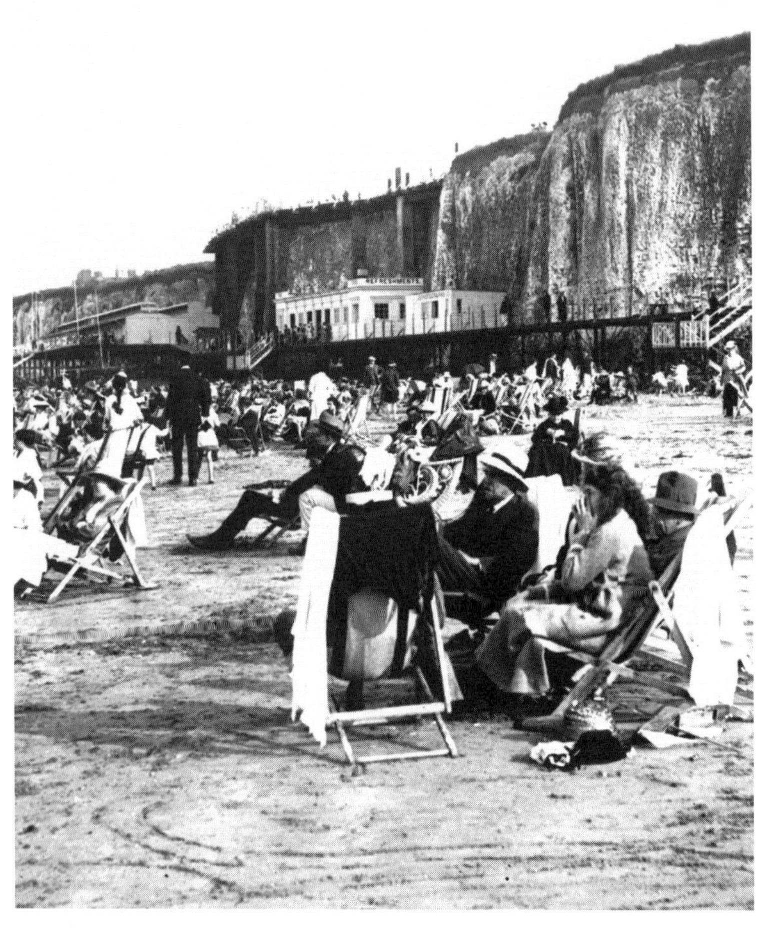

MARGATE

THE SANDS 1918 / 68443

This is a remarkable view—not least because of the 'kreemy toffee' advertised on the left, showing that incorrect spelling has been used in advertising for many years. The 'togetherness' of these Margate beach crowds was legendary; the whole beach was once heard to erupt into song: 'Yes, we have no bananas …'

MARGATE

THE SANDS 1918 / 68454

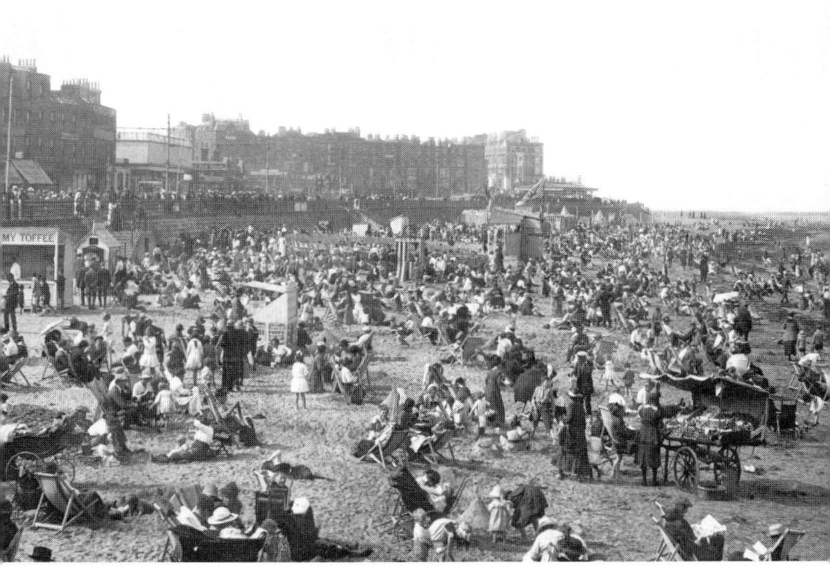

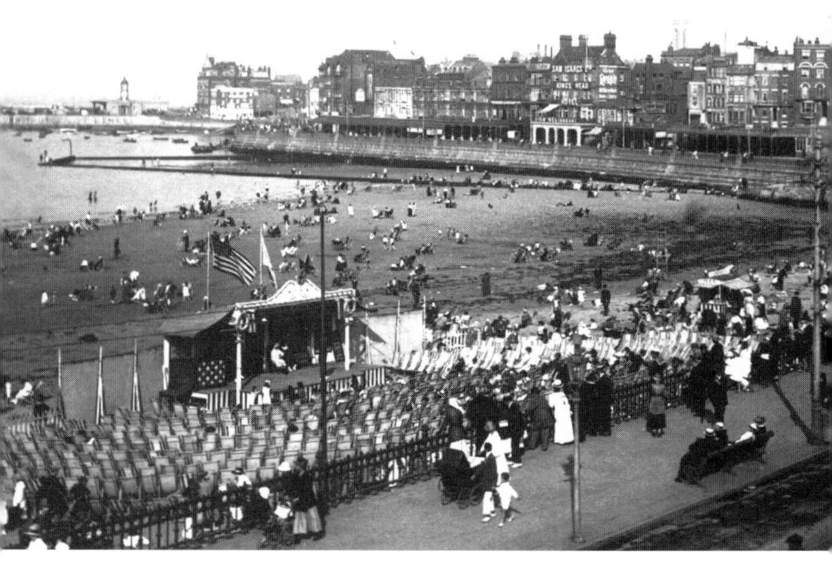

We are looking across the Marine Sands towards Margate Harbour. In the foreground is the well-known and loved theatre on the Marine Sands which opened during the summer months, and featured regular acts such as Gee's Margate Troubadours. The stars and stripes over the theatre suggest American entertainers.

MARGATE

THE SANDS 1918 / 68451

By the late 1920s, not a bathing machine graces the water's edge in this view of the crowded Margate Sands, looking towards the Harbour with the Pierhead Lighthouse.

MARGATE

THE BEACH 1927 / 80344

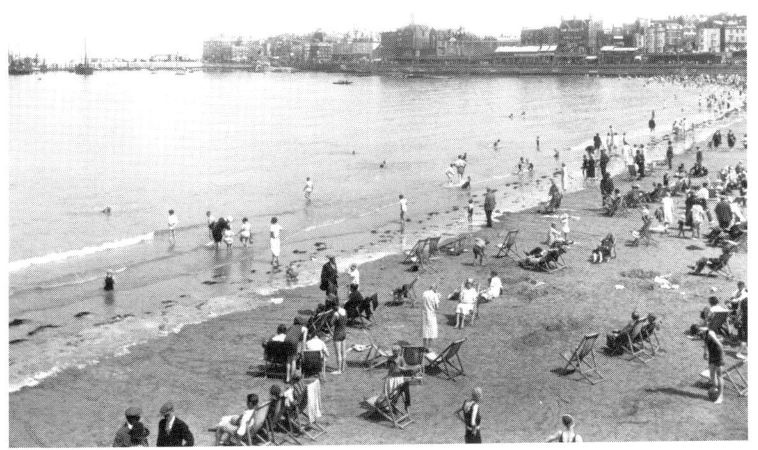

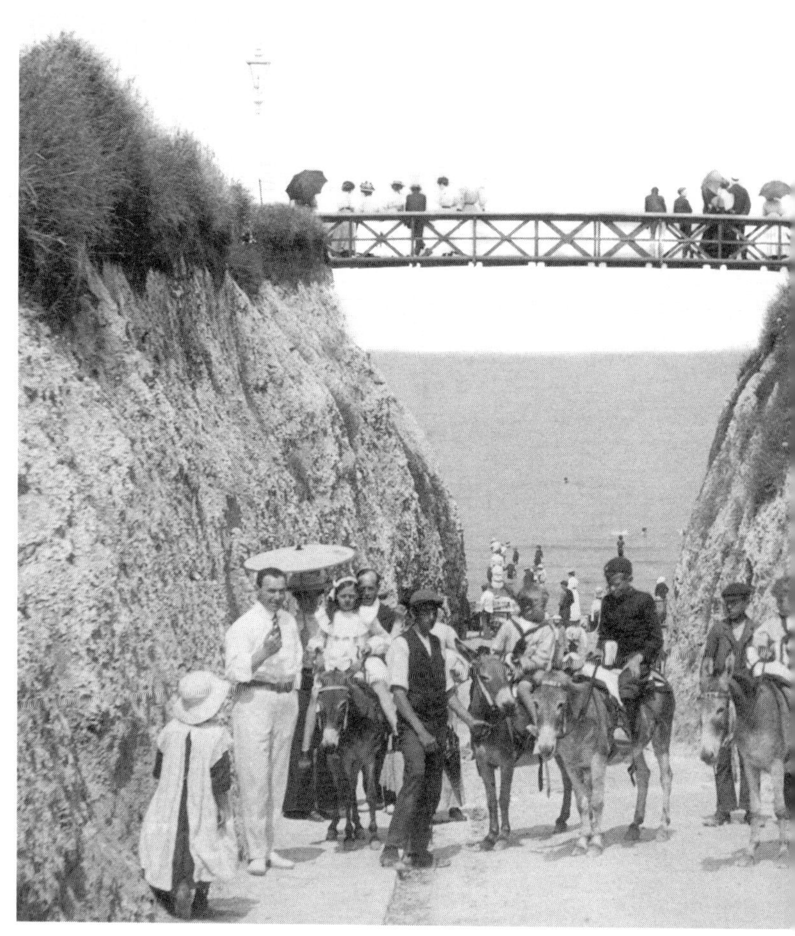

MARGATE

HODGES GAP 1908 / 60372

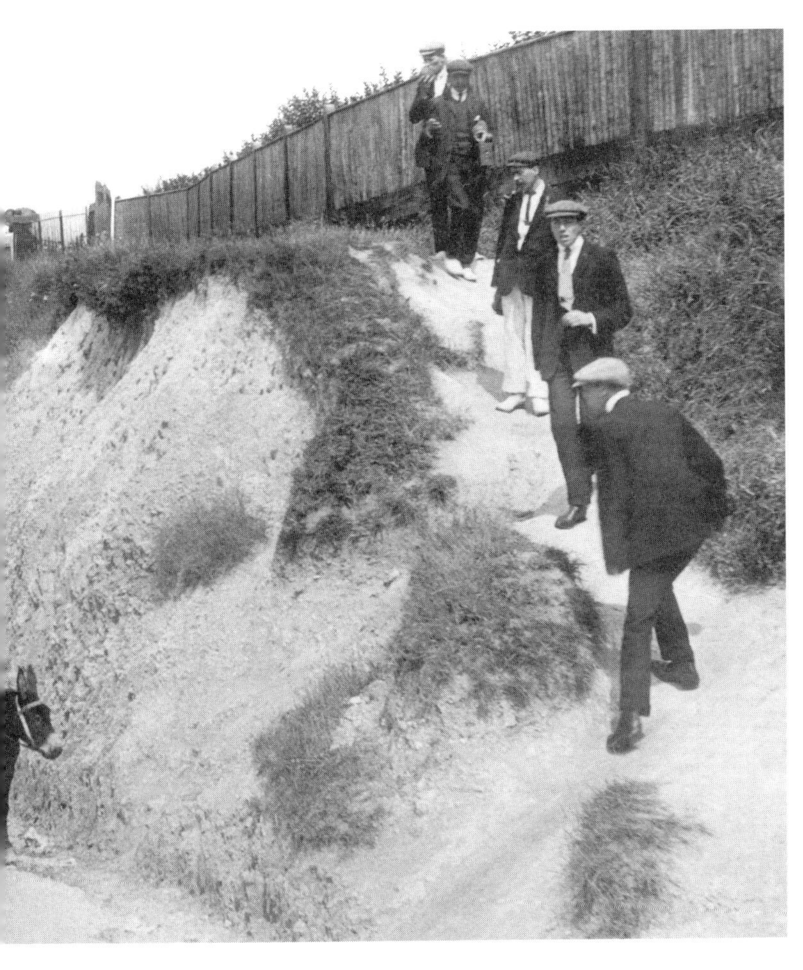

This beautifully-posed view shows the gap through the seacliffs in Cliftonville to the east of Margate. The gap leads down to Walpole Bay and the Bathing Pool. To the east is the flagstaff.

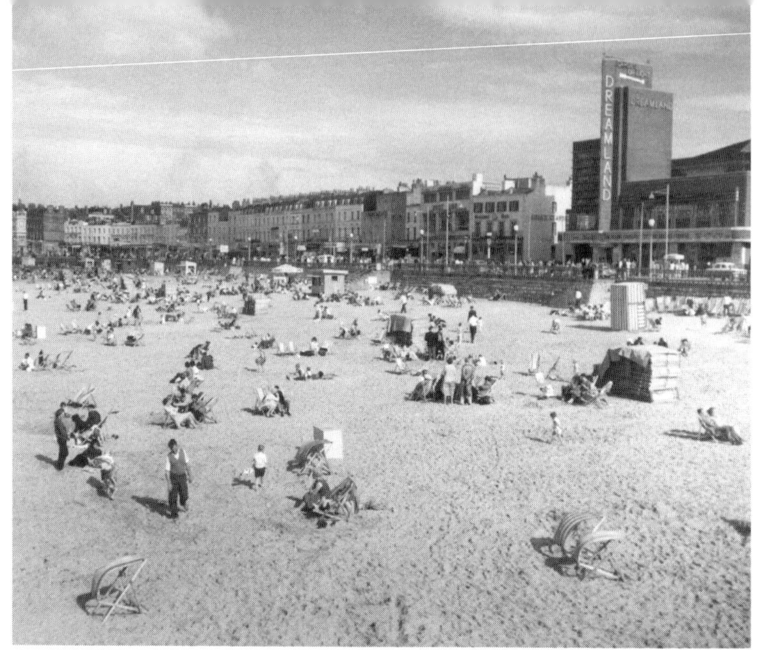

The famous sands are dotted with deckchairs and holidaymakers in the sunshine of the mid 20th century. To the right is 'Dreamland', developed on the site of the famous 'Hall by the Sea' after 1919. Dreamland survives today as a white-knuckle theme park.

MARGATE

THE BEACH C1955 / M31015

MARGATE

THE SURFBOAT MEMORIAL 1906 / 54763

The Surfboat memorial commemorates the nine lifeboatmen who drowned when the surfboat 'Friend of all Nations' was lost on 2 December 1897. The memorial was erected in October 1899. The disaster, which happened only a few hundred yards from the shore, shocked all Margate.

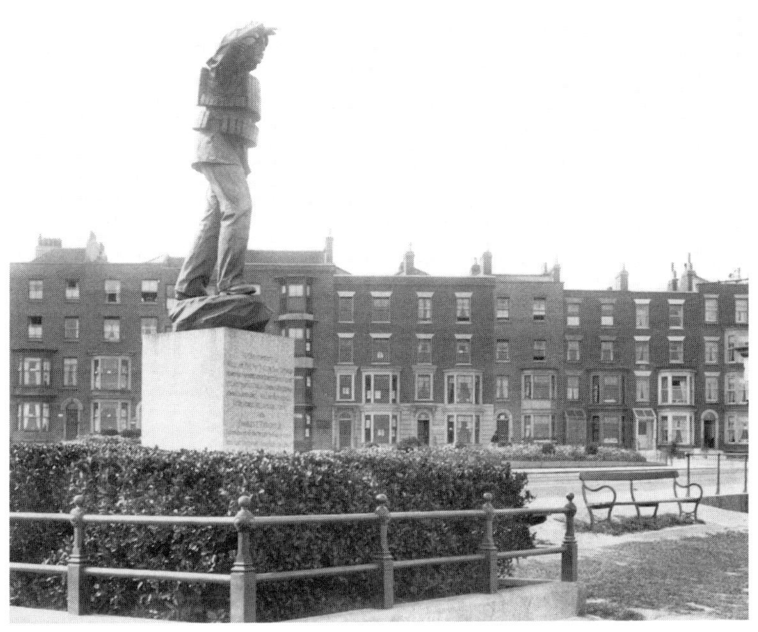

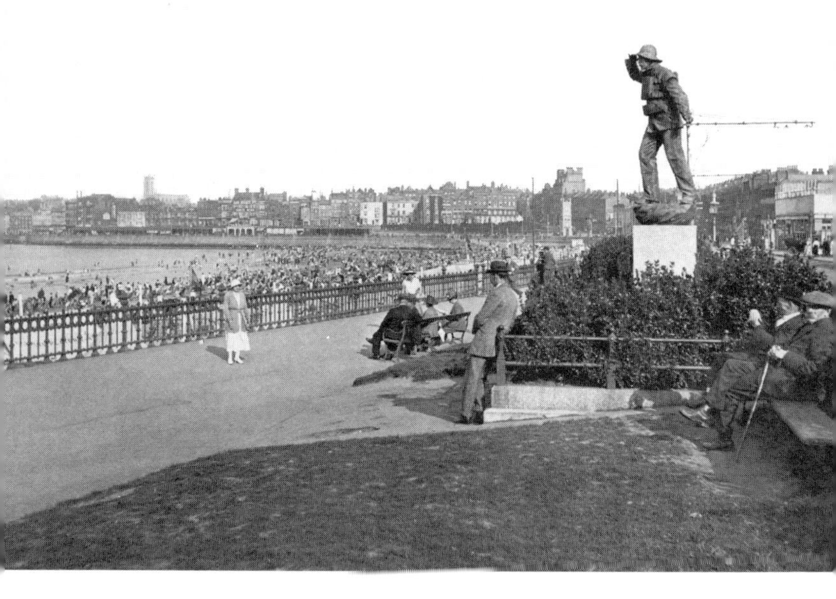

The monument shows a lifeboatman looking out towards the Nayland Rock where the 'Friend of all Nations' capsized when answering distress signals from the 'Persian Empire'.

MARGATE

THE SURFBOAT MEMORIAL 1918 / 68452

It is low tide at Margate Harbour, with fishing boats lying in the mud. The Droit House, Pier Hotel (later the Metropole) and the Ship Hotel are visible on the left. The pier was built in 1810-1815 of Whitby stone, and is 909 ft long. It replaced an earlier structure destroyed by a big storm in 1808.

MARGATE

THE HARBOUR c1865 / 2721

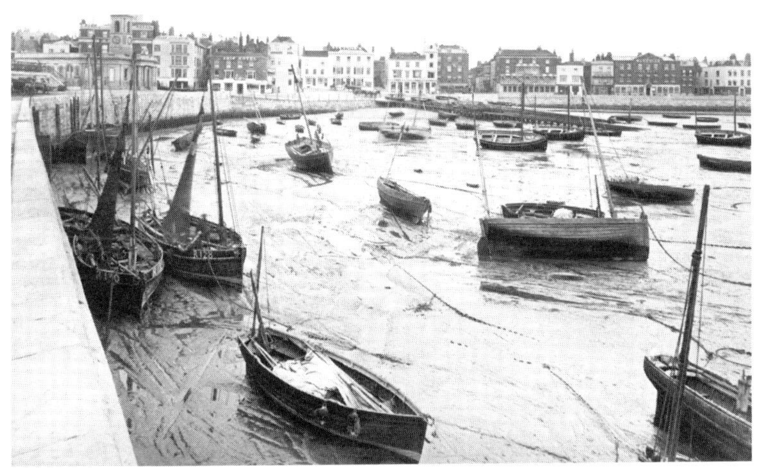

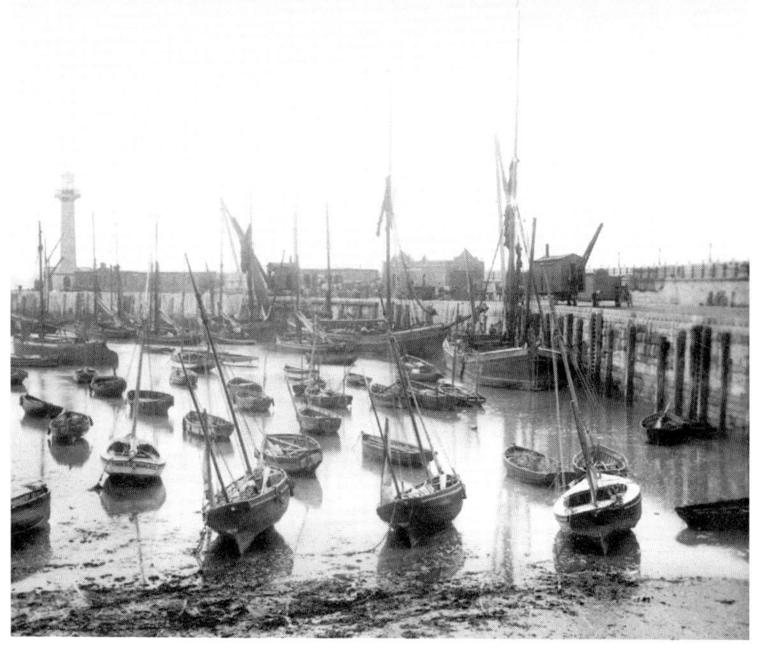

Another low-tide photograph of Margate harbour. Several sailing barges involved in coastal trade are moored close to the pier. Wagons can be seen on the pier railway. On the left is the Pierhead Lighthouse.

MARGATE

THE HARBOUR 1906 / 54762

MARGATE

THE HARBOUR 1908 / 60370

Sailing barges are moored in the harbour, with the Lighthouse in the centre of the picture. The harbour was originally important not just for the coasters and fishing traders, but as the place of arrival and departure of trippers from London. They came originally in the famous Margate 'hoys', and later by steam packet.

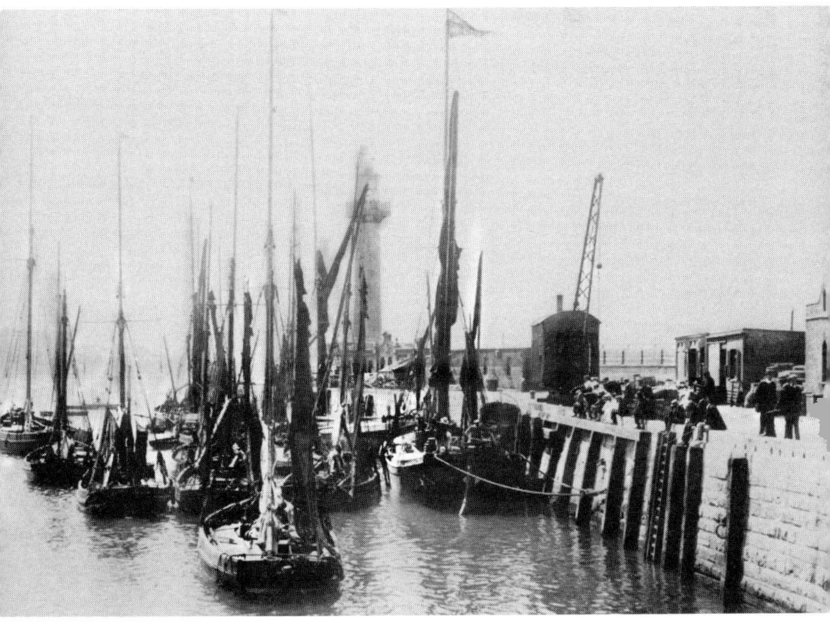

We are looking back towards the Parade and Marine Terrace from the Harbour Pier, with fishing boats and pleasure craft afloat on the rippling water. A tablet on the Pier commemorates nine seamen of Margate lost in 1857 when the 'Victory', a lugger, went to the assistance of the American vessel 'Northern Belle', which came ashore on the Foreness Rock near Kingsgate.

MARGATE

THE HARBOUR C1955 / M31008

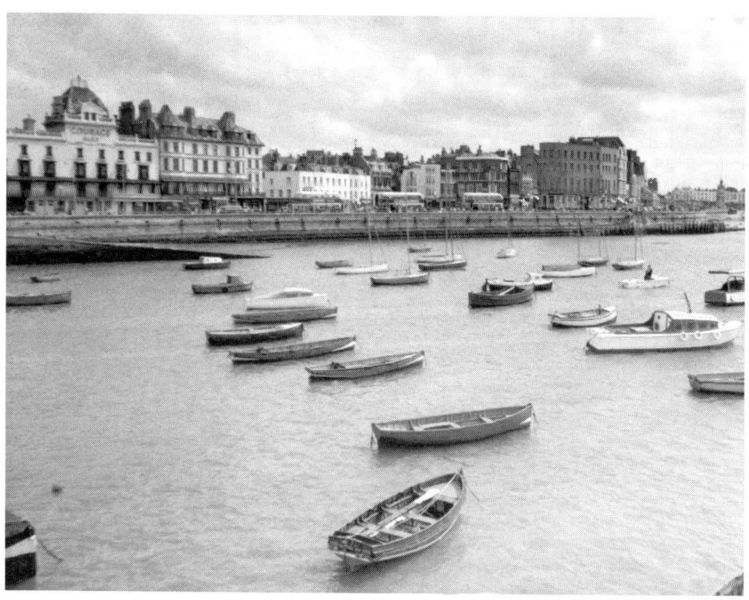

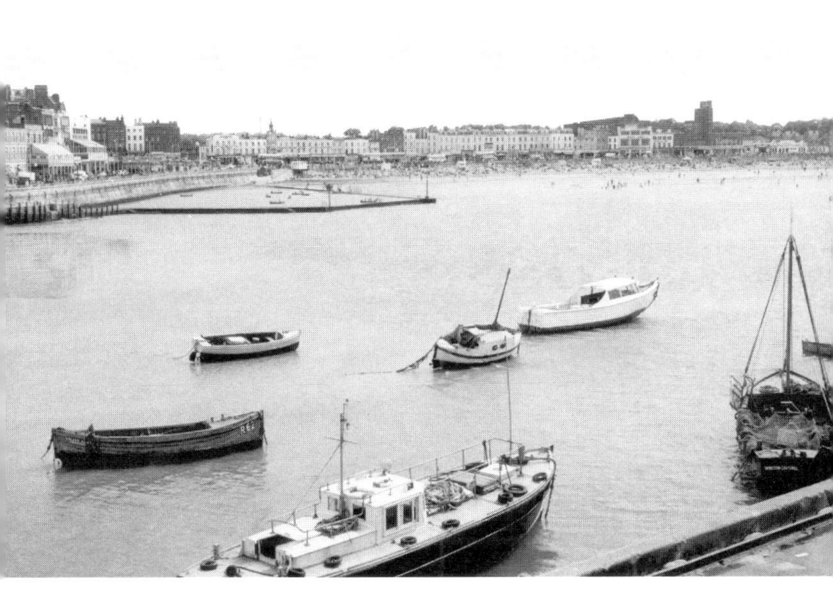

This view looks across the harbour and the boating pool from the pier. The clock-tower is just to the right of the centre of the picture, and we can see the entrance tower to the Dreamland amusement park. This is the oldest theme park in Kent, which today puts emphasis on white knuckle rides - though some of the gentler rides of 60 years ago still remain in operation.

MARGATE

MARINE TERRACE FROM THE LIGHTHOUSE c1965 / M31006

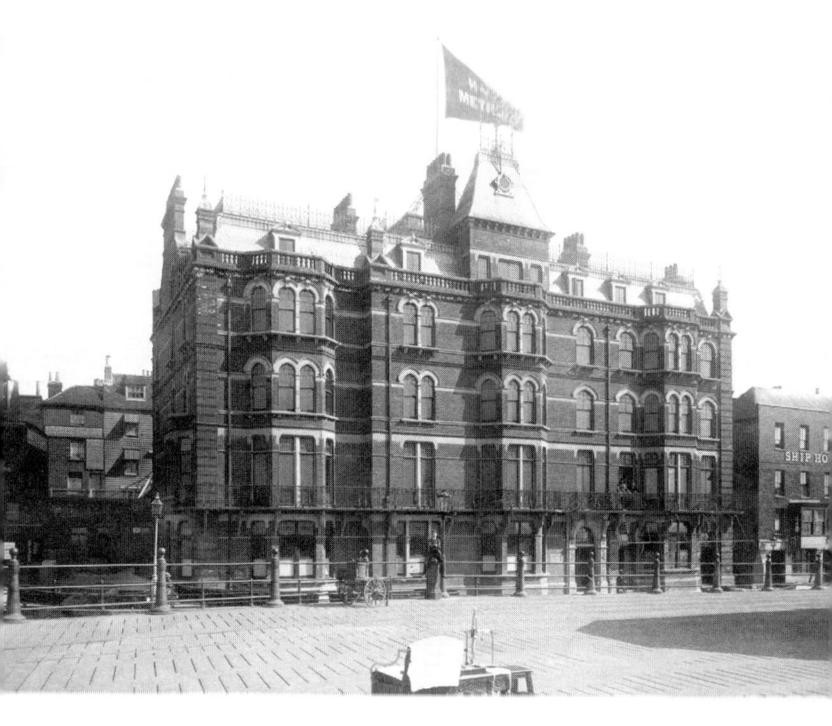

Built as the Pier Hotel in 1891, the Metropole stood at the landward end of the jetty. It was demolished, along with the adjacent buildings including the Ship Hotel, in 1938 to make way for Fort Hill and the Rendezvous.

MARGATE

HOTEL METROPOLE 1892 / 31443

We are looking east along Queen's Promenade: fashion parades in the sun by the sea. Cliftonville has always been the more 'select' quarter of Margate, and is still a very popular residential area.

MARGATE

CLIFTONVILLE, QUEENS PROMENADE 1908 / 60374

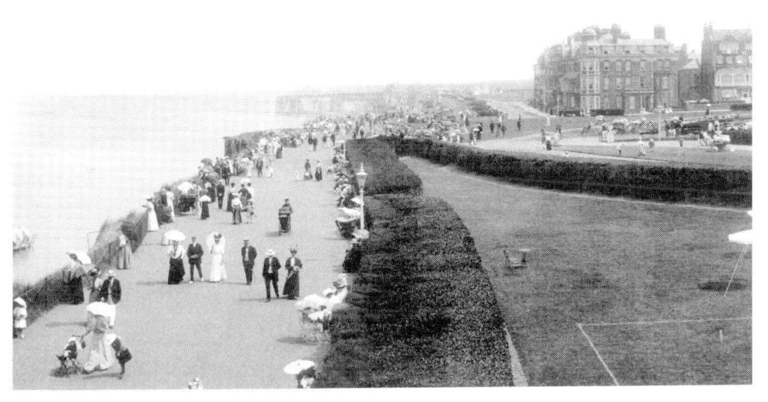

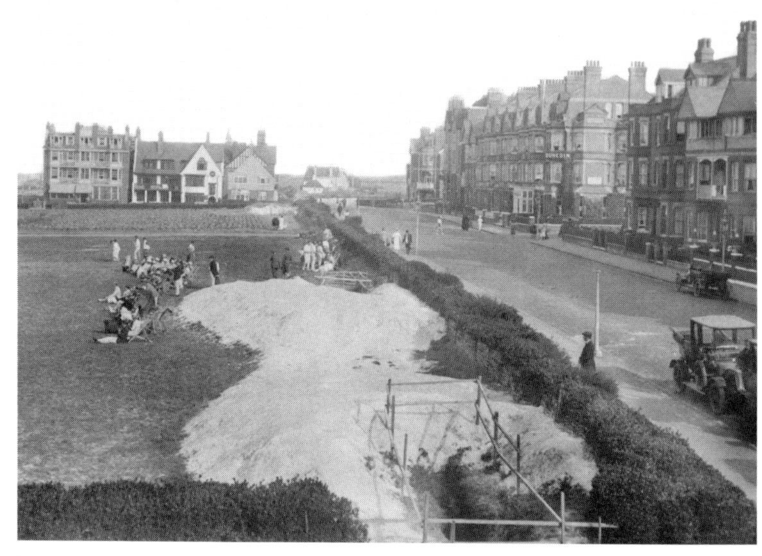

The Lawns, Cliftonville's rectangular-shaped cliff-top open space, with its bowling greens and seats high above the sea, is shown here some ten years after picture 60374 was taken, possibly in the last summer of the First World War.

MARGATE

CLIFTONVILLE 1918 / 68435

MARGATE

ST JOHN'S CHURCH 1890 / 27445

St John's is Margate's parish church. It contains 12th-century arcades, which accounts for its long low profile; St John's has been considerably rebuilt over the years, and was extensively restored in 1875 by Christian. The 14th-century tower and spire seen in this picture had been rebuilt to a greater height by Christian.

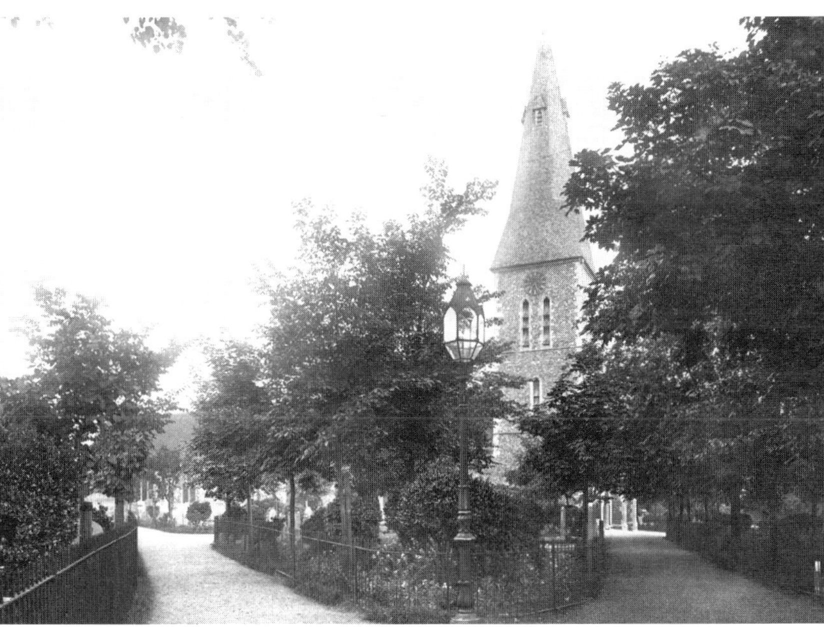

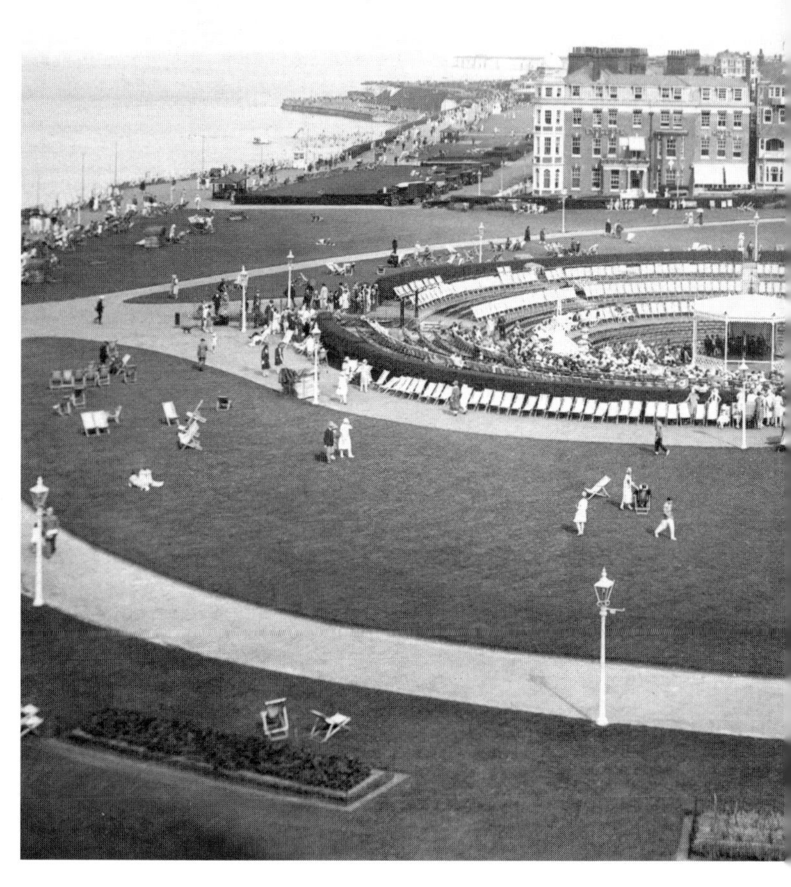

MARGATE

CLIFTONVILLE, THE OVAL 1927 / 80352

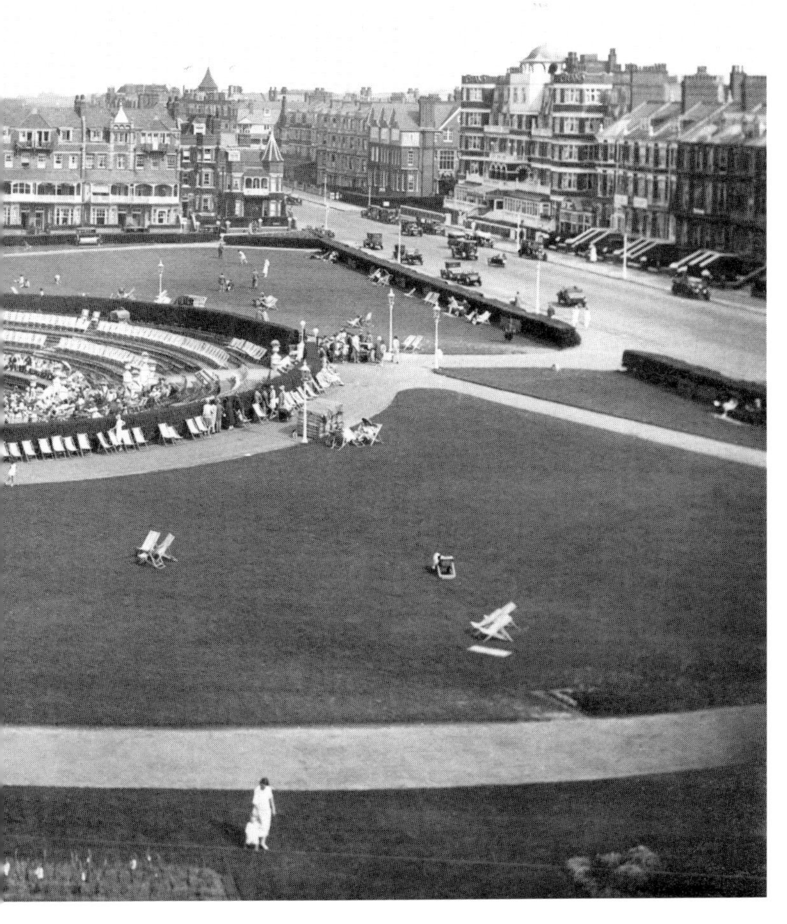

Cliftonville's Oval, with its sunken bandstand, is seen here between the wars. Daily concerts are held with deck-chairs arranged in circles around the bandstand.

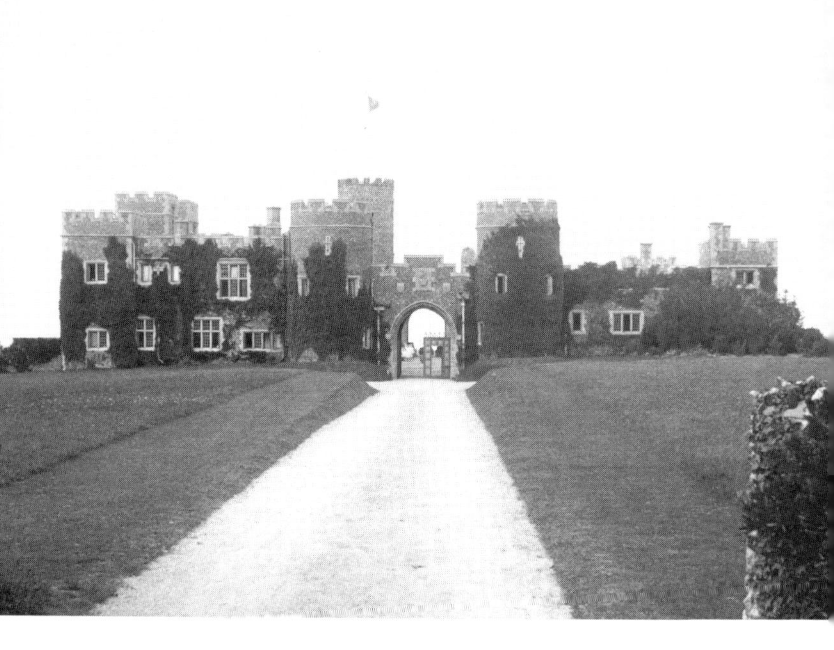

Kingsgate Castle was built in about 1860 close to the sea cliff's edge and the North Foreland itself. It is shown here romantically clothed in ivy. At this time it was the home of Lord Avebury, the distinguished author, scientist and inventor of the bank holiday. It became a hotel in 1922, and was later converted to 32 flats.

KINGSGATE

THE CASTLE 1908 / 60382

Kingsgate stands at the gap in the cliffs closest to the North Foreland. Its present name dates back to 1683 when Charles II landed here—it was formerly St Bartholomew's Gate. This picture looks towards the castellated Victorian pile of Kingsgate Castle, with the white houses of Kingsgate Bay Road on the right. The largest of these is Holland House, built for Lord Holland in the 1760s, but now much altered.

KINGSGATE

THE CASTLE 1908 / 60381

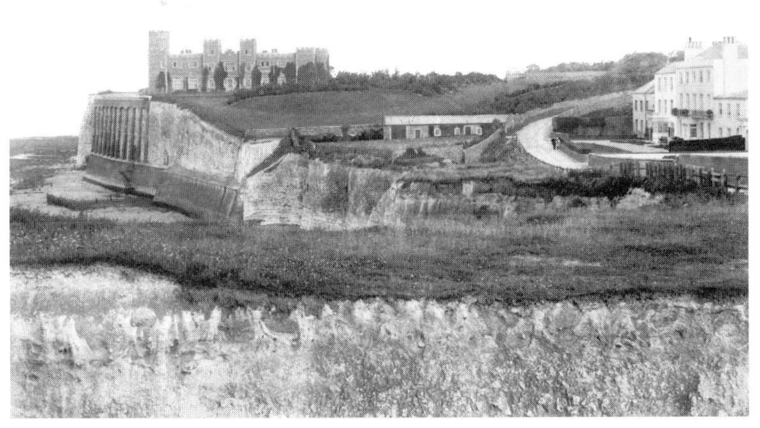

This view looks towards Kingsgate Castle—now cleaned of its ivy—some 60 years after the above photograph was taken. On the right is the entrance to the steps down to the sandy beach of Kingsgate Bay.

KINGSGATE

THE CASTLE c1965 / K124041

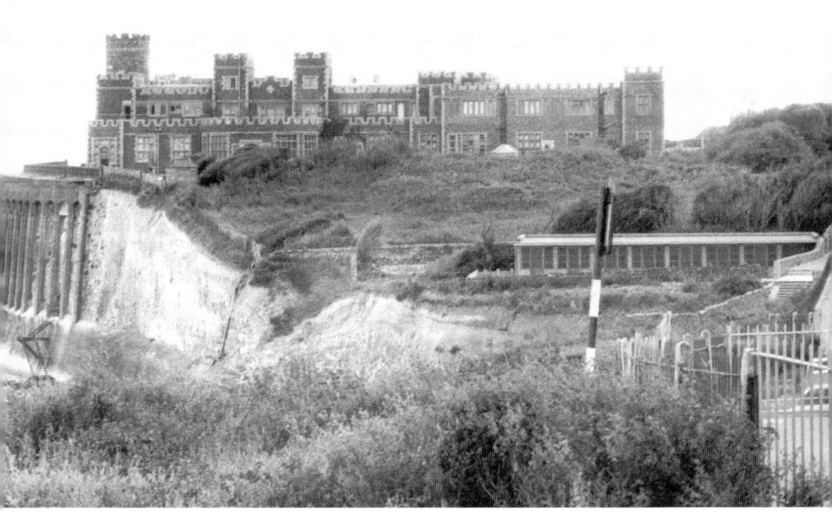

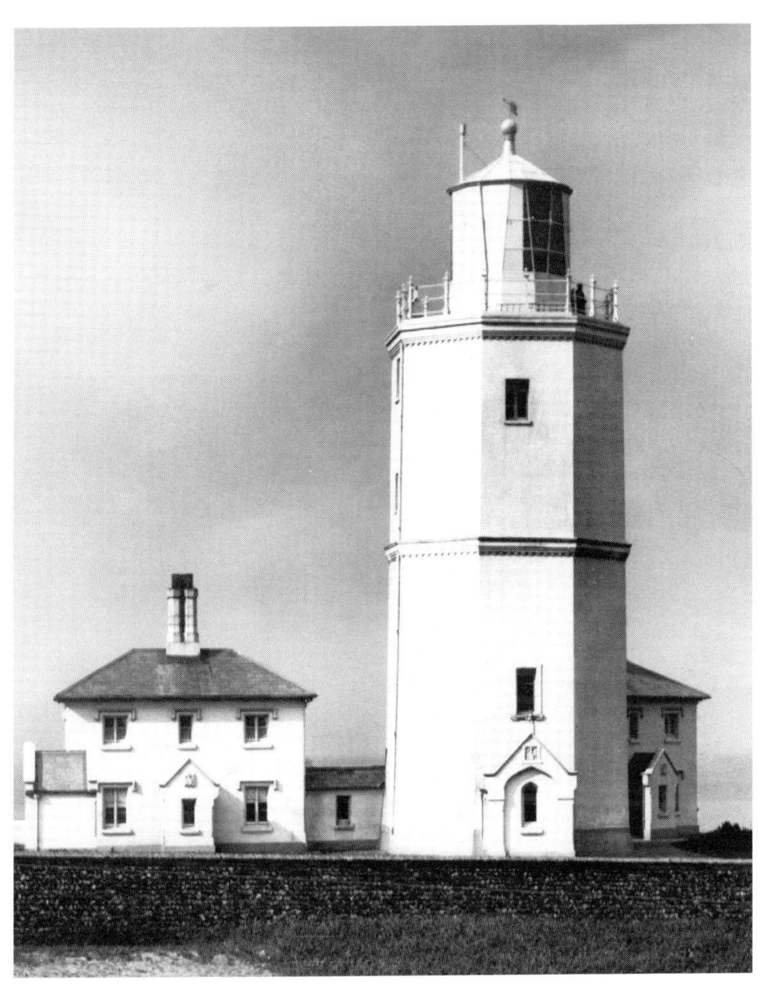

BROADSTAIRS

THE NORTH FORELAND LIGHT 1887 / 19728

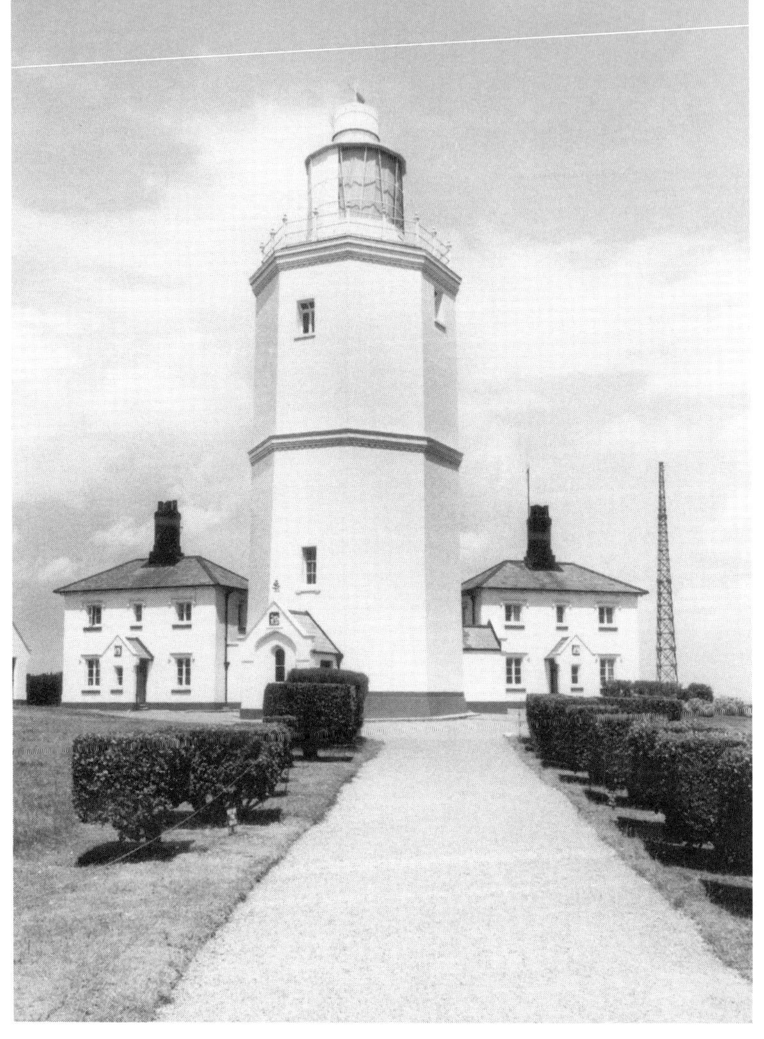

BROADSTAIRS

THE NORTH FORELAND LIGHTHOUSE C1965 / B220032

The 85-foot high functional-looking white tower of the North Foreland Lighthouse was built in the late 17th century. The light, 188 feet above high water, is visible for 19 miles. There is said to have been a lighthouse here since 1515. It was here, off the Foreland in 1666, that the English fleet engaged the Dutch in a four-day-long sea battle, 'the longest and most stubborn that the seas have seen'.

BROADSTAIRS

THE NORTH FORELAND LIGHTHOUSE 1894 / 34192

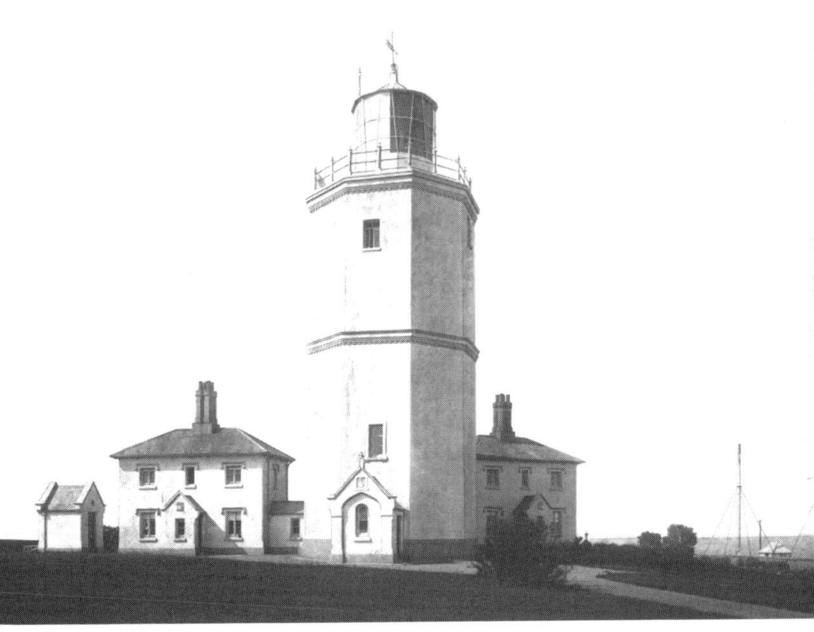

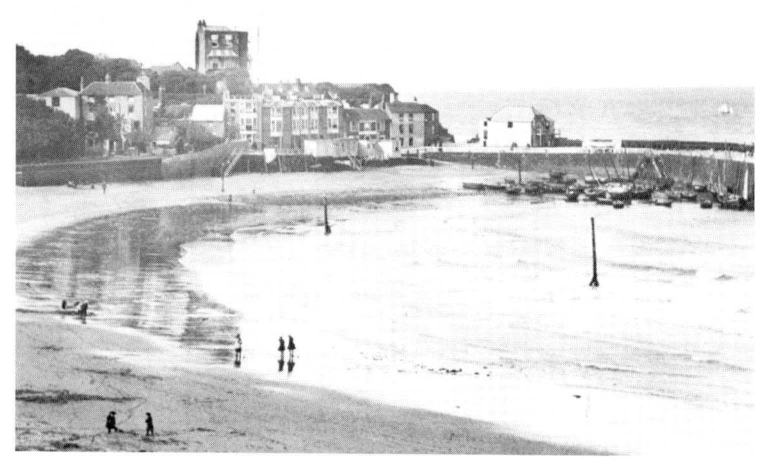

We are looking across Main Bay (now Viking Bay) towards the harbour, the pier and the prominent mansion Fort House (now called Bleak House), prior to its extension and castellation in 1901. This house was Dickens' summer residence in 1850, and here he completed 'David Copperfield'. The old pier, which dates from 1808, stands on the site of a Tudor pier destroyed by storms.

BROADSTAIRS

THE HARBOUR 1887 / 19707

BROADSTAIRS

THE BEACH AND THE HARBOUR C1960 / B220015

This is a similar view to photograph number 19707, but taken some seventy years later. On the left is Bleak House, now castellated, and on the right the pier and little harbour. Broadstairs retains its Dickens association with its annual Dickens Festival.

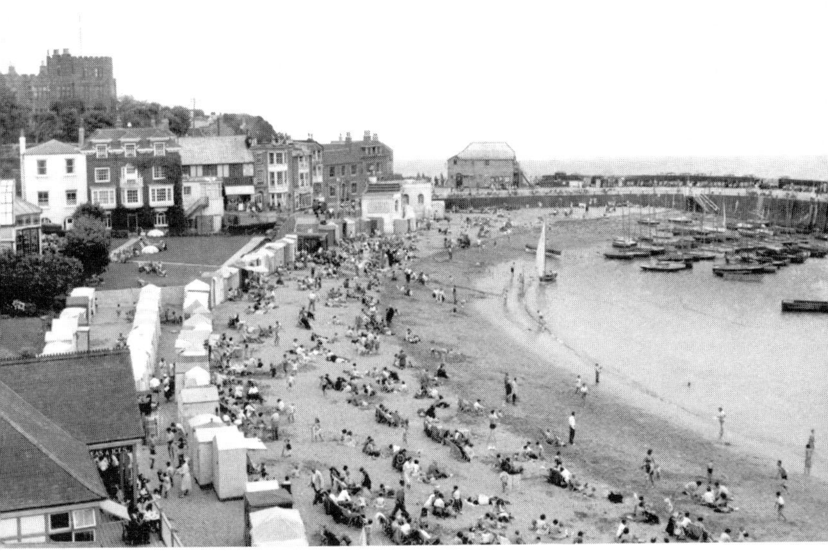

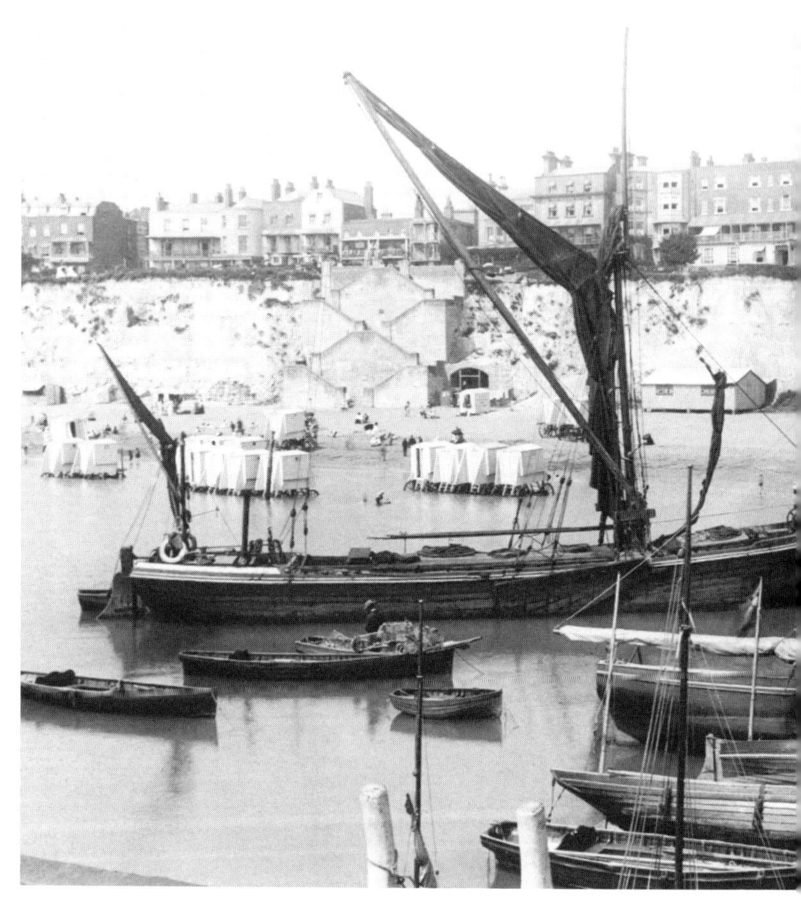

BROADSTAIRS

THE HARBOUR 1897 / 39592

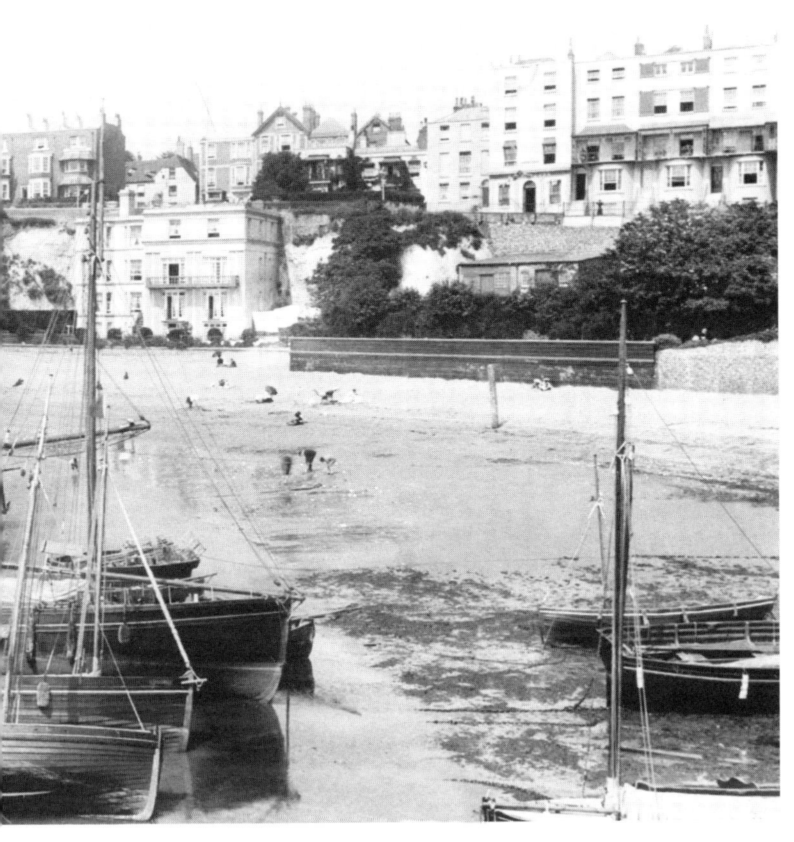

Fishing boats and a Thames sailing barge—probably a collier—fill the foreground of this picture, which was taken from the pier. Broadstairs was described at the time of this photograph as 'quieter and more select than its larger and noisier neighbours'. The house at beach level in the centre of the picture is Eagle House (the House on the Sands).

This view looks across the Main Bay from the pier, with two Thames sailing barges in the centre of the picture. Note the line of bathing machines under the cliffs. In former days, Broadstairs was noted for the shrine of 'Our Lady of Bradstow', so venerated by sailors that they would dip their sails in salute as they passed.

BROADSTAIRS

THE HARBOUR 1902 / 48845

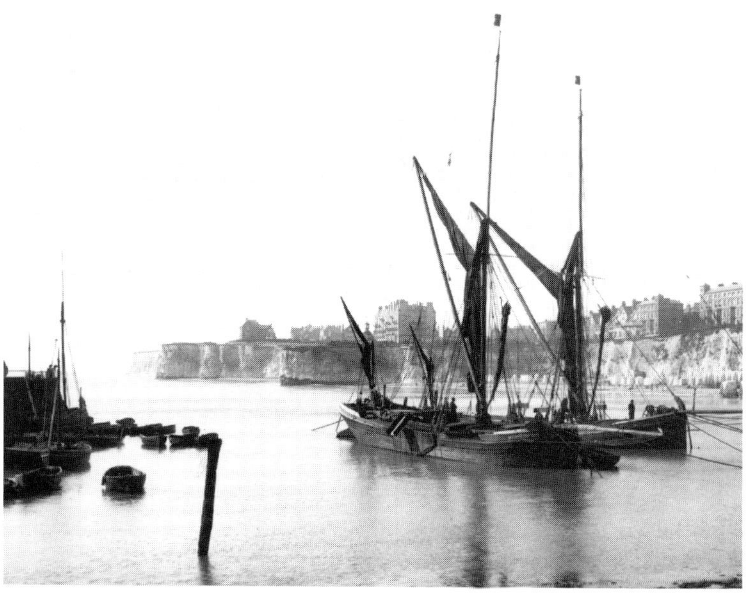

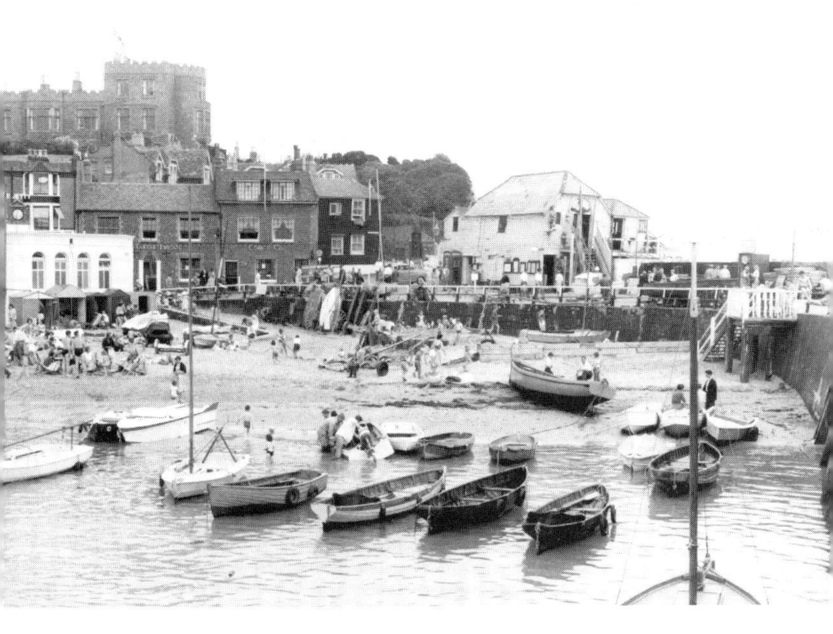

Fishing boats and pleasure boats crowd the harbour close under the pier, while holiday-makers throng the beach. In the centre is the well-known harbour inn, The Tartar Frigate, while Bleak House looks down over the holiday scene.

BROADSTAIRS

THE HARBOUR c1965 / B220056

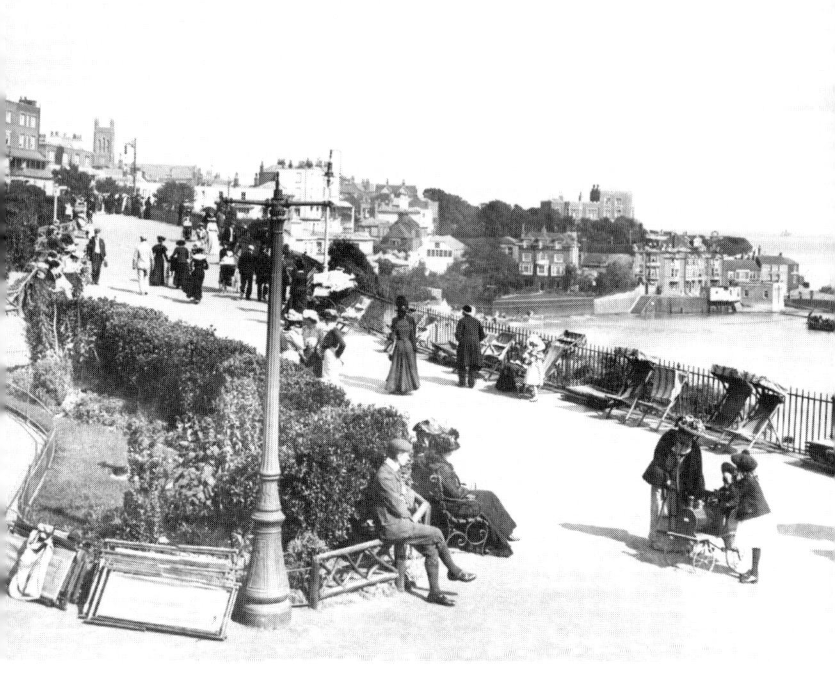

The Promenade above Main Bay (Viking Bay) overlooks the harbour; Edwardian promenaders are taking the air. Bleak House stands on the right, while on the left is the prominent tower of Holy Trinity church, built in 1862. Note the canopied deckchairs on the right.

BROADSTAIRS

THE PROMENADE 1902 / 48842

Holiday-makers are scattered across the sands in this evocative picture. The famous steps to the beach are visible on the right. The bandstand is in the centre on the cliff top, and the Grand Hotel is on the left.

BROADSTAIRS

THE SANDS 1899 / 44217

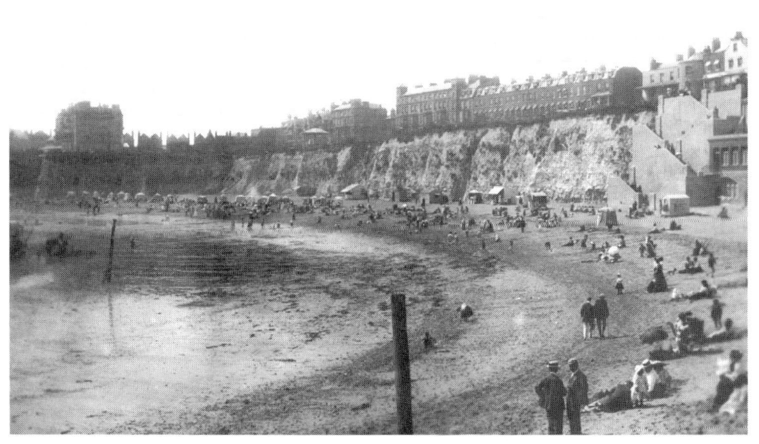

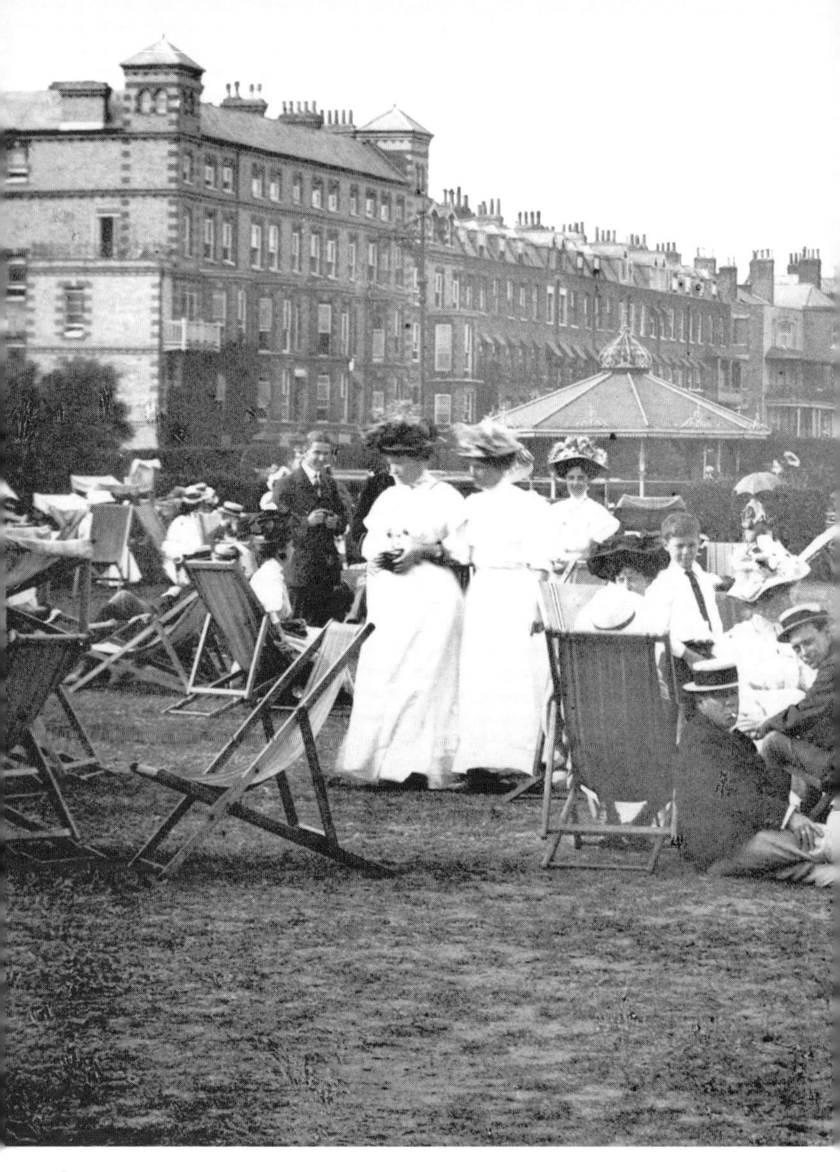

BROADSTAIRS

THE BANDSTAND 1907 / 58329

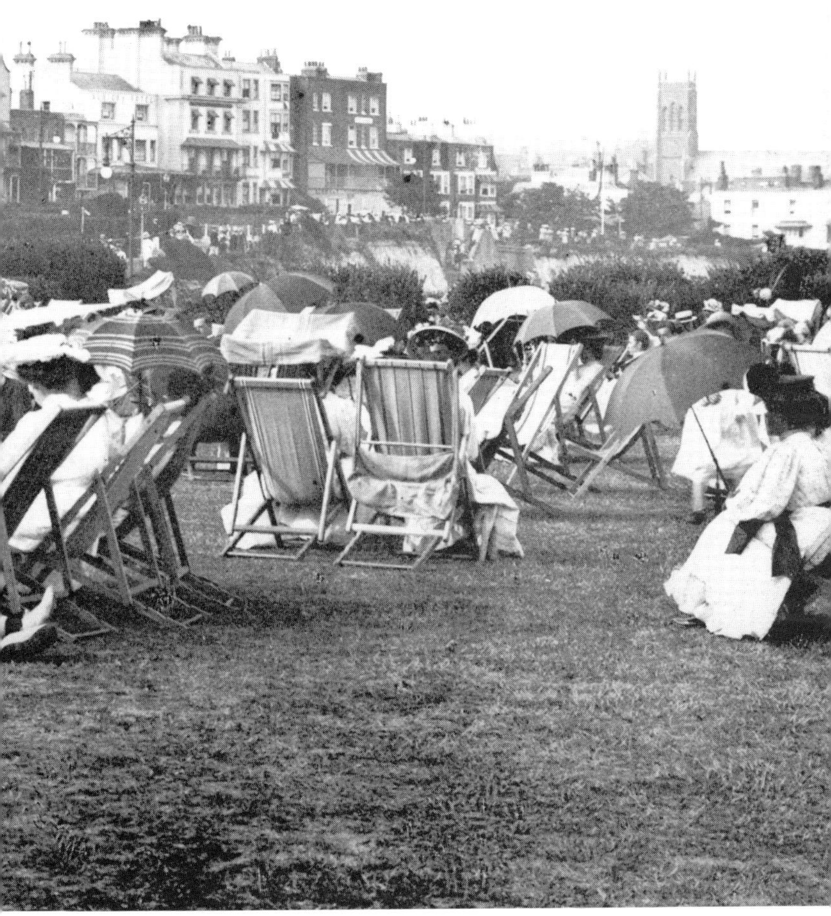

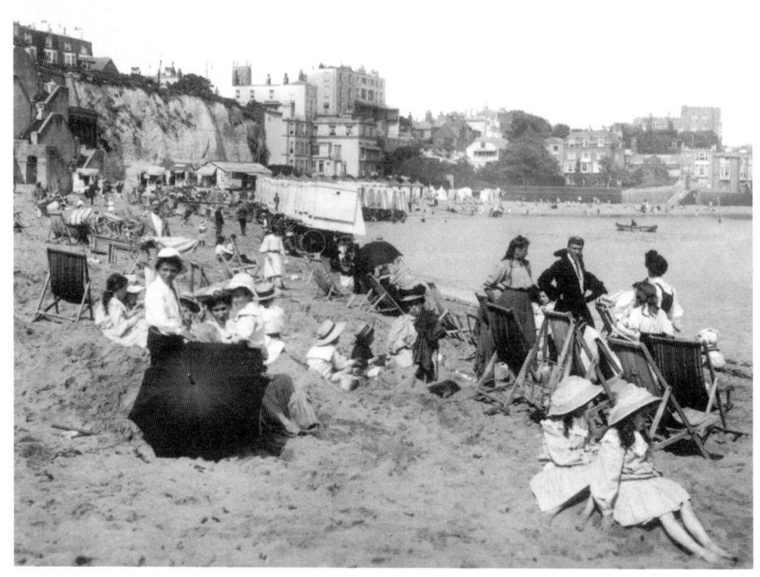

All the familiar seaside fun is here: happy holiday-makers digging in the sand, deckchairs and bathing machines fill this evocative picture of Edwardian Broadstairs. The steps and the lift house are on the left, Eagle House in the centre and Bleak House on the right.

BROADSTAIRS

THE BEACH C1907 / 58327

BROADSTAIRS

THE SANDS 1912 / 65021

In a brisk breeze, bringing white-crested waves to the beach, the holiday crowds enjoy the sands at Broadstairs. Note the boy in a sailor suit on the left and the donkey on the right.

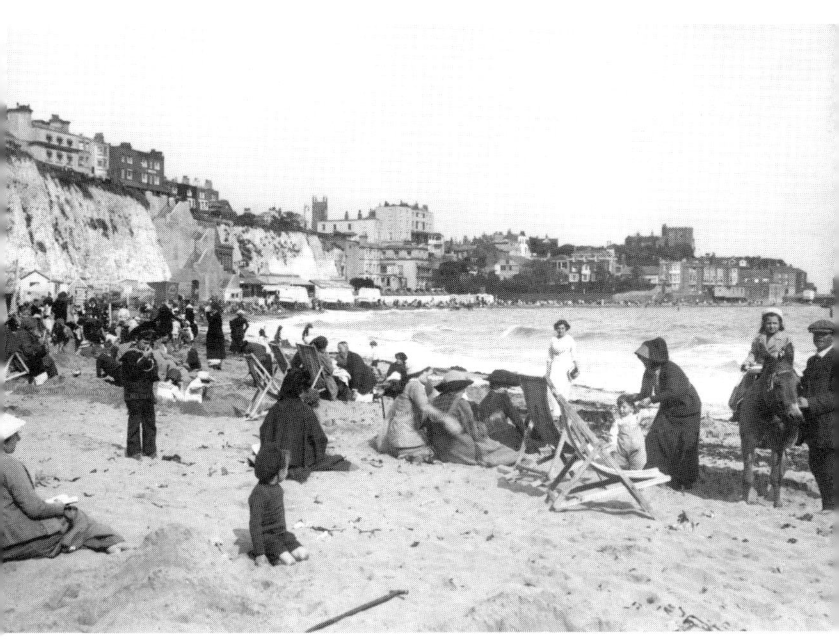

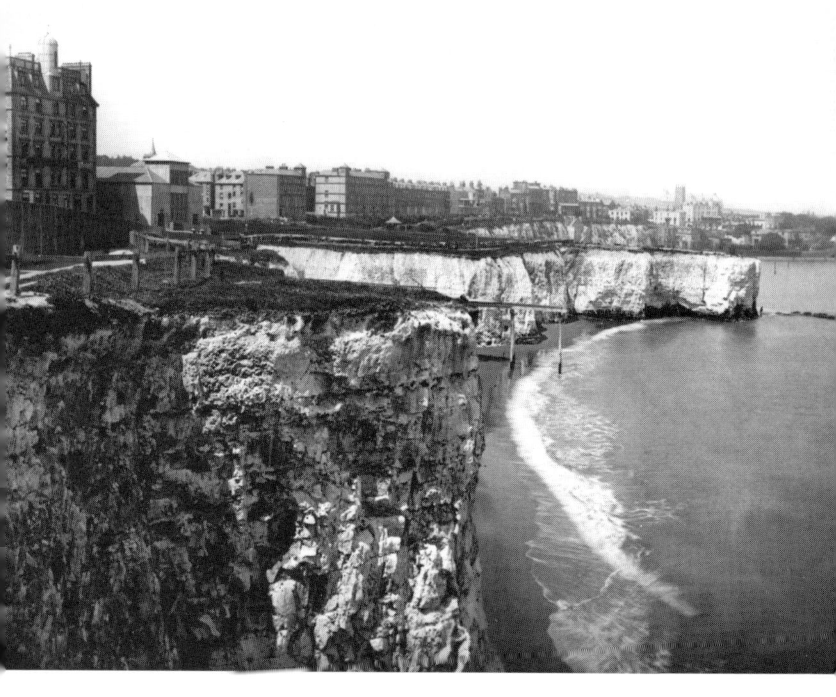

The chalk cliffs of the coast at Broadstairs show superbly in this late Victorian view, looking across Louisa Bay and Viking Bay towards the harbour, in the days before any coastal protection work had been undertaken. The present sea wall was not built until the 1960s.

BROADSTAIRS

VIEW FROM THE CLIFFS 1887 / 1970s

Bathing tents dot the beach at Viking Bay, while two bathing machines stand at the water's edge. At the time of this picture, Broadstairs was 'especially in high favour with family parties who find quite a little paradise in its sheltered beach'. The main steps to the promenade and Victoria Parade are in the centre of the picture.

BROADSTAIRS

FROM THE CLIFFS 1897 / 39589

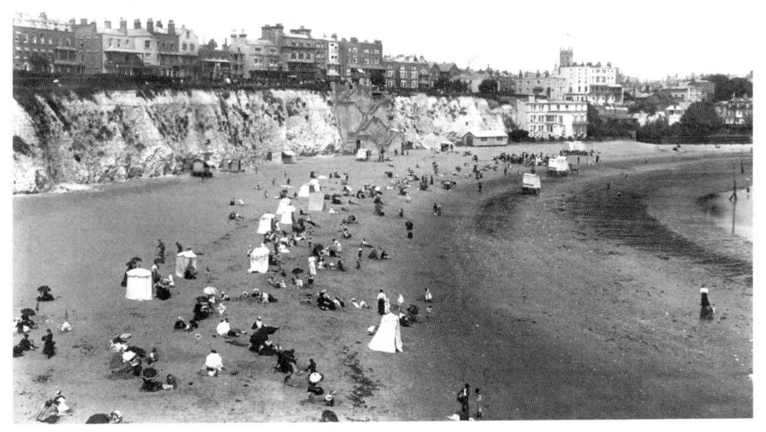

The Victorian bulk of the Grand Hotel looms over Louisa Bay; this photograph shows how the clifftop had become increasingly built-up. Since then, a protective sea wall has been built in a bid to arrest coastal erosion.

BROADSTAIRS

THE GRAND HOTEL AND THE CLIFFS 1899 / 44211

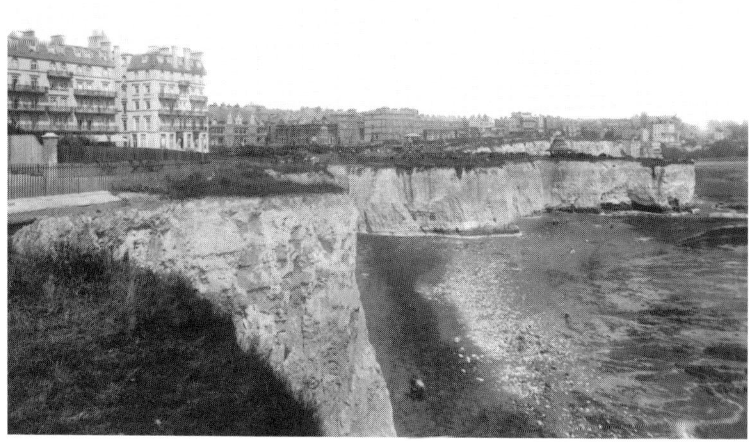

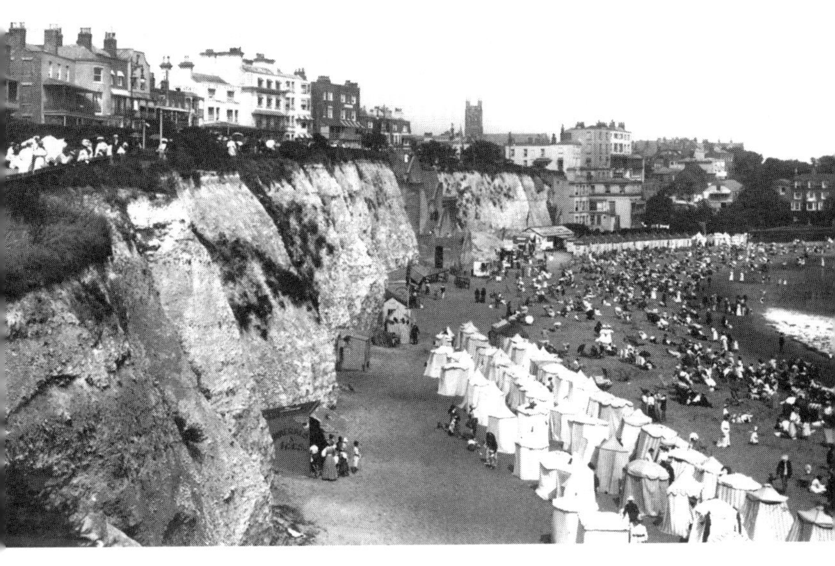

Serried ranks of bathing tents and a crowded beach spell out summer fun at Broadstairs during the early twentieth century. Note the kiosk selling minerals and ices at the foot of the cliff on the left.

BROADSTAIRS

THE BEACH 1907 / 58325

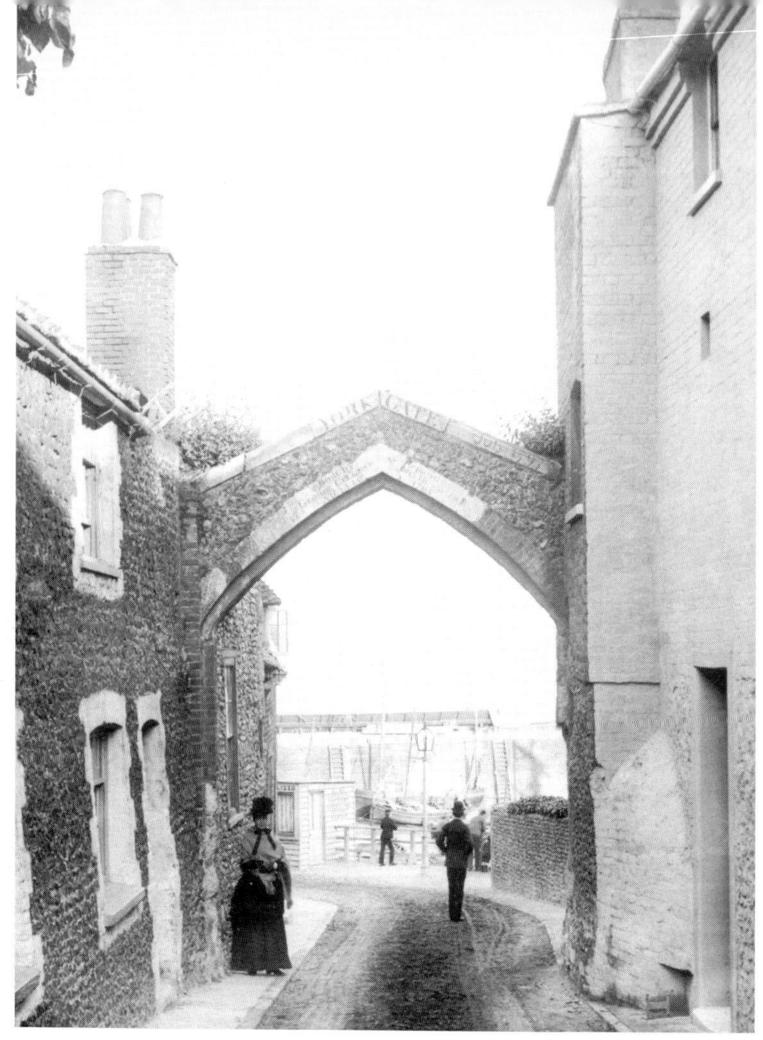

BROADSTAIRS

YORK GATE 1887 / 19726

The attractive old streets of St Peters are still one of the most delightful aspects of Broadstairs. It was traditionally much more important than its 'little suburb by the sea', and was included in the jurisdiction of the Cinque Ports.

BROADSTAIRS

ST PETER'S CHURCH 1897 / 39587

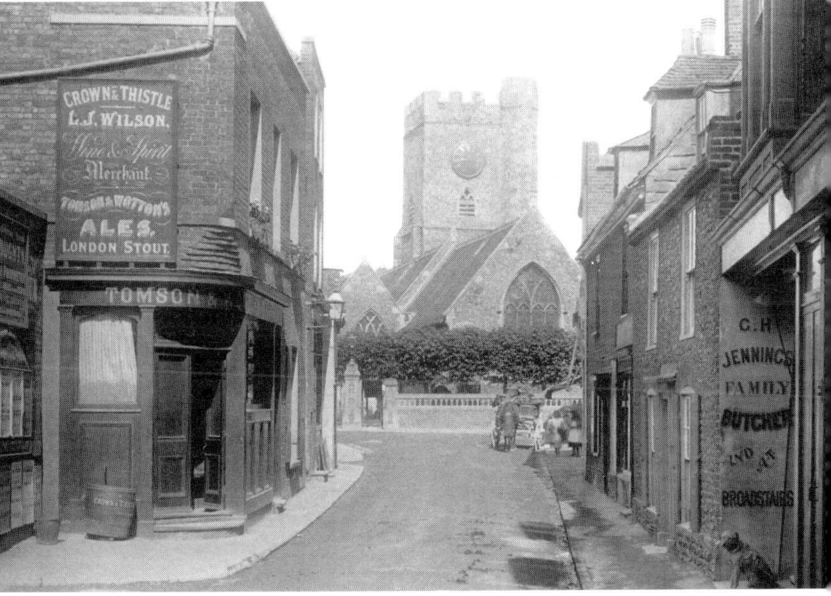

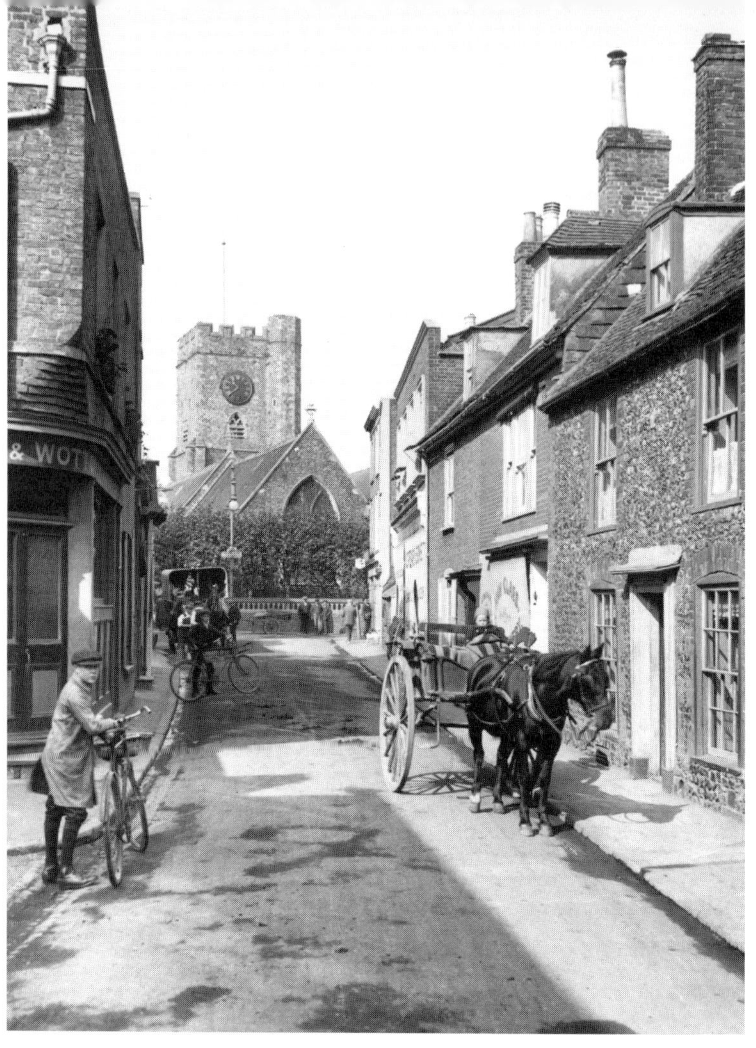

BROADSTAIRS

ST PETER'S 1912 / 65029

RAMSGATE

NELSON CRESCENT 1894 / 34199

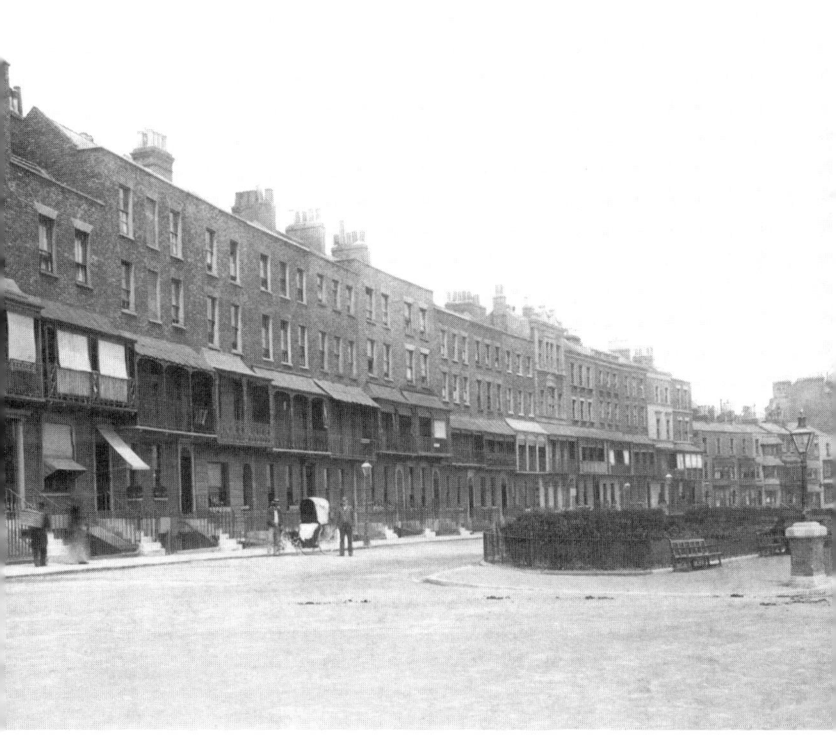

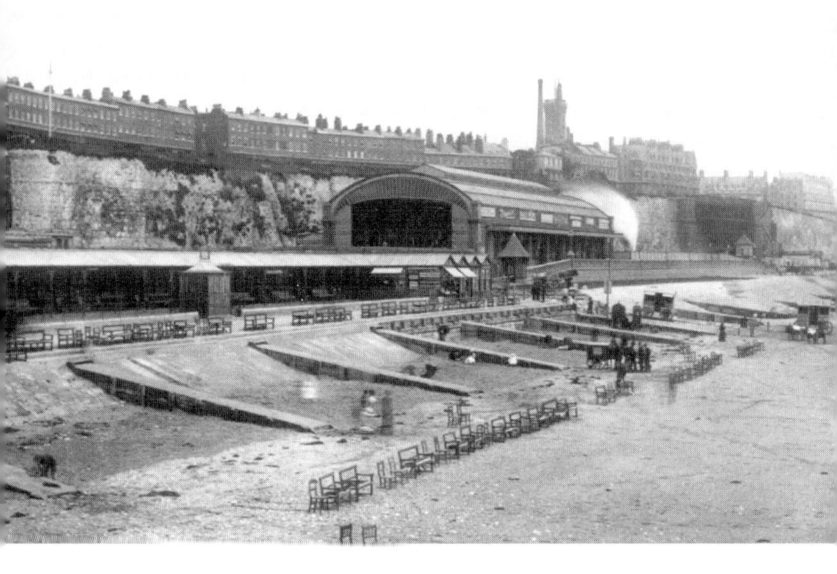

This early picture of the beach at Ramsgate shows the benches that were precursors of the modern deck chair and a few bathing machines. Ramsgate Sands Station is in the centre of the picture. It was one of two stations at Ramsgate, and was the terminus of the London, Chatham and Dover Railway. It opened in 1863 and closed in 1926.

RAMSGATE

THE BEACH c1880 / 12731

Here we see a very crowded Ramsgate beach, with the pier in the distance on the right beyond the massed bathing machines. Note the large number of beach vendors, and the dark-rooms of two rival photographers in the centre of the picture.

RAMSGATE

THE BEACH 1907 / 58272

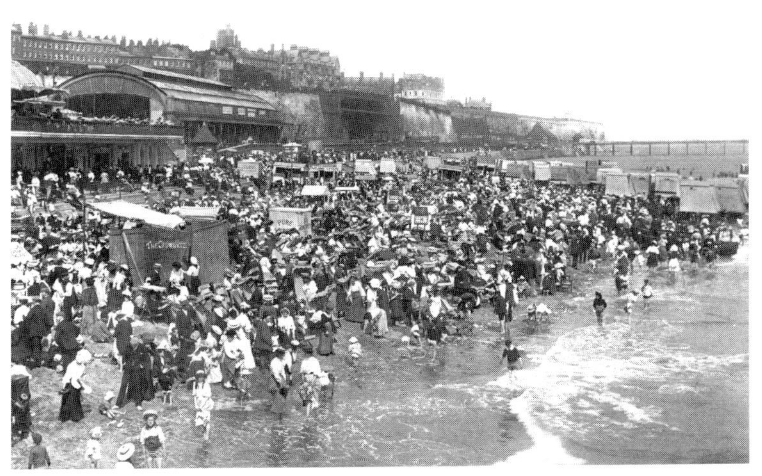

We are looking towards the inner harbour-now the yacht marina—with a paddle steamer and three brigs at moorings. The chimney on the left of the Admiral Harvey pub probably belonged to Ramsgate's first gasworks, run by a local chemist.

RAMSGATE

FROM WEST CLIFF 1887 / 19674A

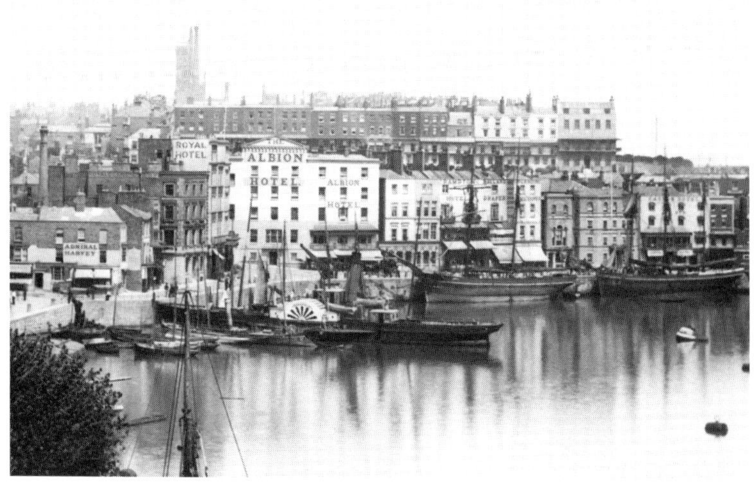

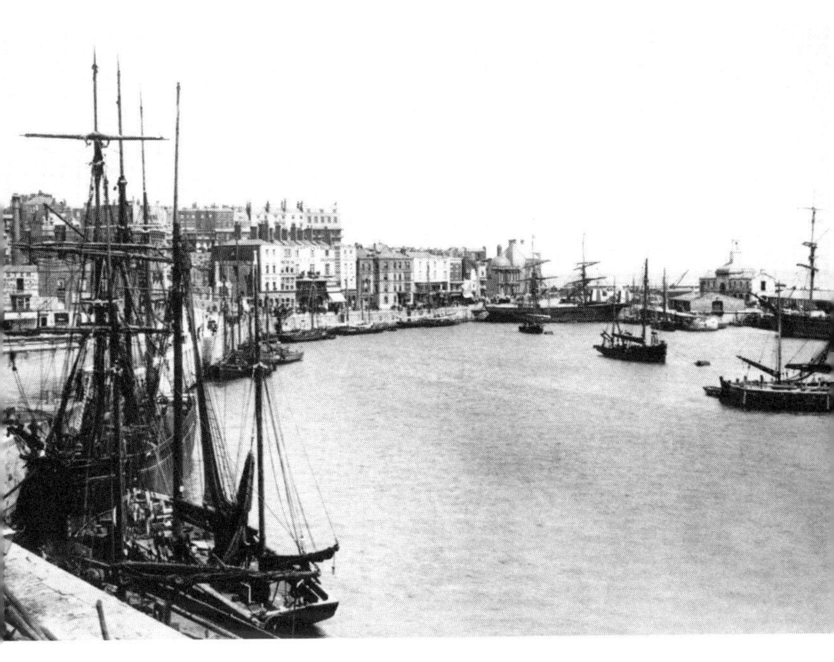

The harbour is packed with an assortment of sailing craft, including fishing smacks, brigs and sailing barges. During the 1880s, Ramsgate had the largest fishing fleet in south-east England-144 vessels all told. The premises of W T Foster's ship's chandlery, founded in the 1870s, is on the left.

RAMSGATE

THE HARBOUR 1895 / 35871

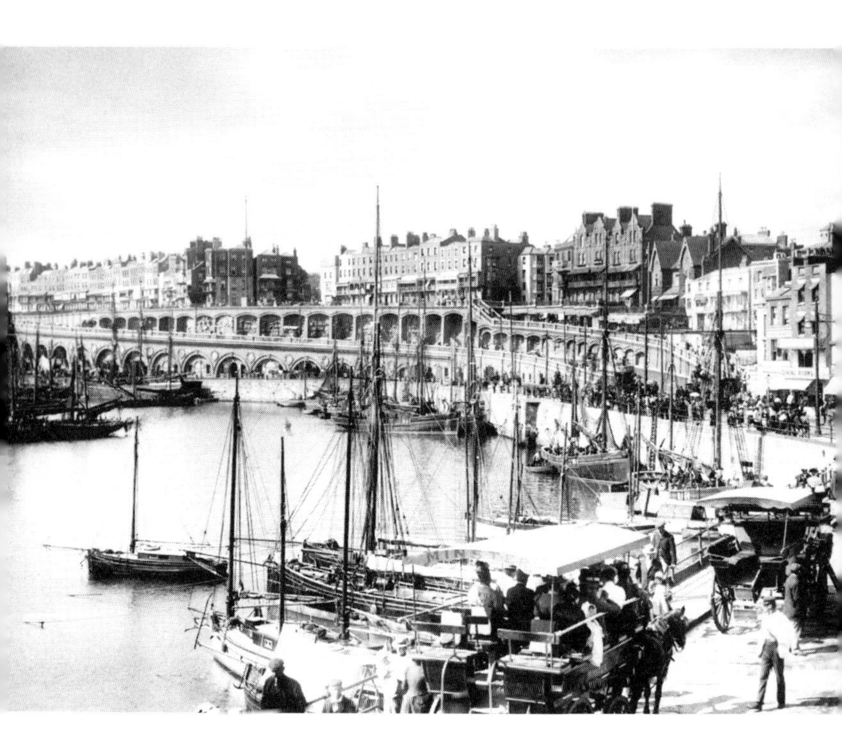

Plenty of shipping is in the harbour, with part of the famous fishing fleet. During the 1890s the convict ship 'Success' was moored here. She carried prisoners to Australia. The horse-drawn brakes in the foreground were used by sightseers.

RAMSGATE

THE HARBOUR 1901 / 48028

During the mid 20th century the forest of masts had vanished from Ramsgate's harbour, giving it a very different appearance to earlier pictures. It is interesting to reflect that the inner harbour is now the yacht marina.

RAMSGATE

THE INNER HARBOUR c1955 / R7013

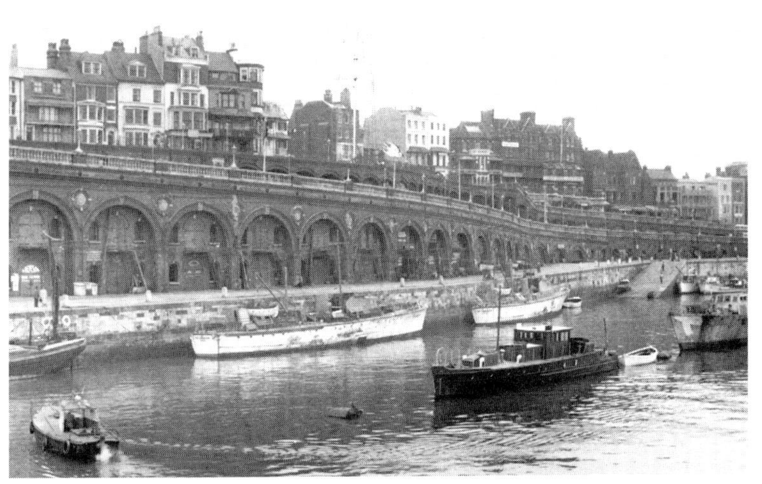

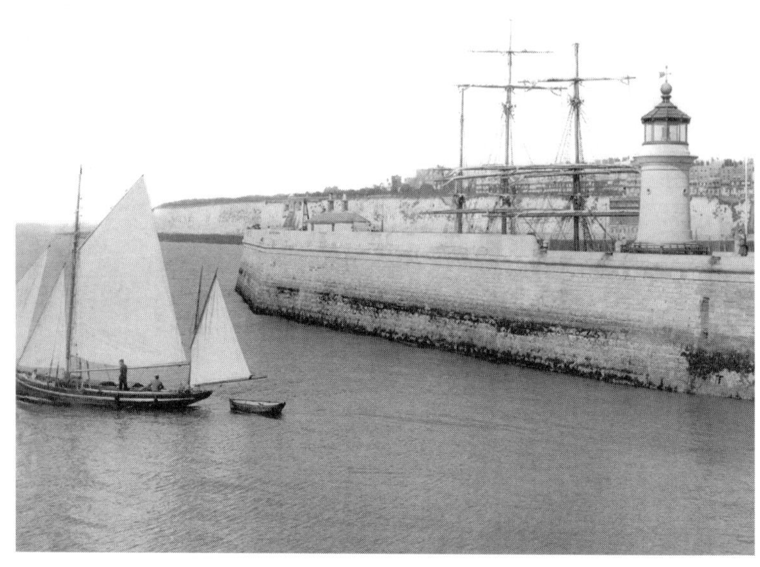

Outward bound from Ramsgate harbour, with a good view on the left of the West Pier and the lighthouse (note the masts of the sailing vessel moored in the harbour). The lighthouse was designed by John Shaw and was first lit in 1842. Ramsgate's harbour was constructed in 1749-91 following a disastrous storm. Its main architect was John Smeaton (the builder of Eddystone lighthouse), who first employed the diving bell for constructing foundations here.

RAMSGATE

THE LIGHTHOUSE 1901 / 48035

RAMSGATE

UNDERCLIFFE 1907 / 58287

This very interesting picture shows, in the centre, the fishmarket of 1881, which was demolished in the 1960s. On the left are colliers unloading—note that the coal is being transferred to horse and cart. On the right is the famous clock house.

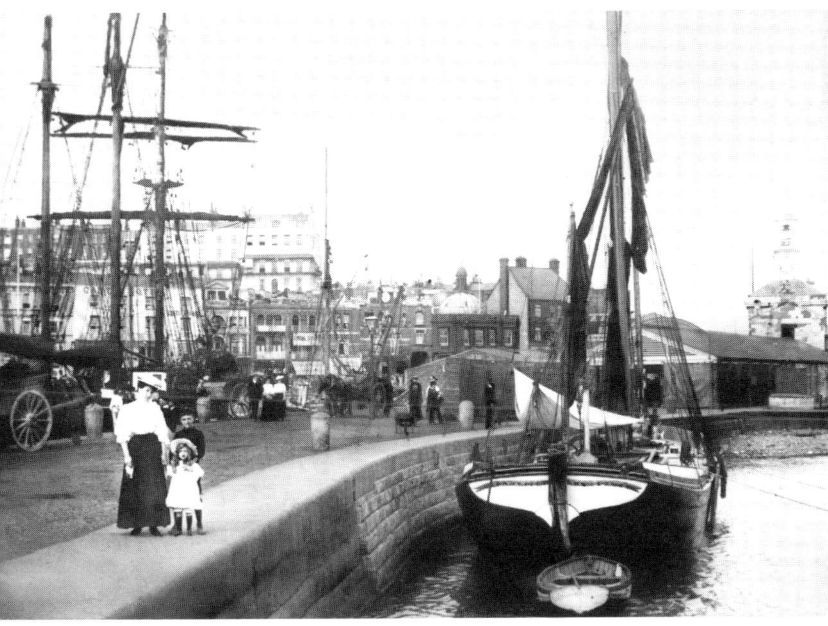

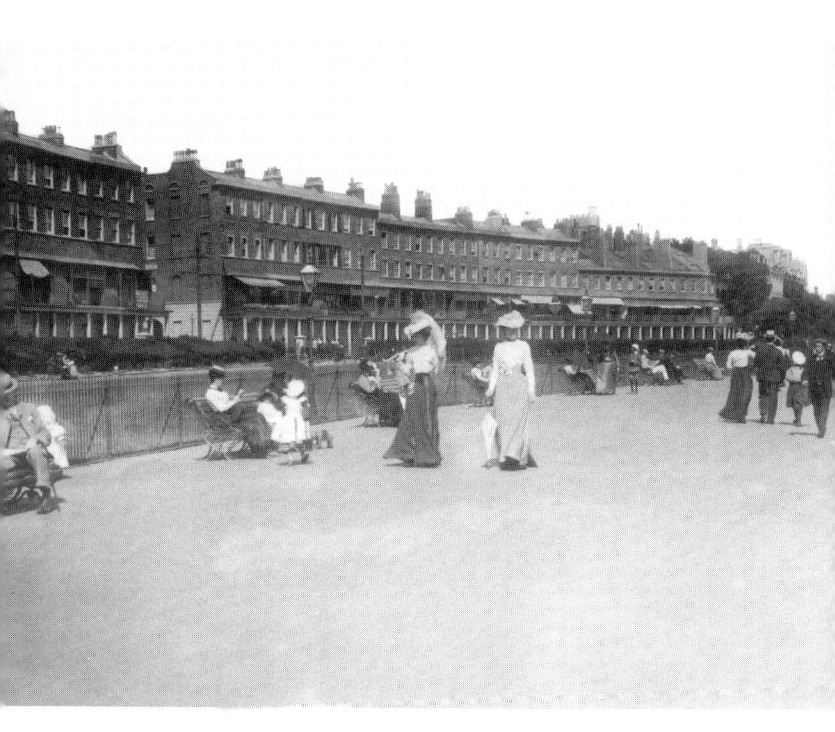

Fashions are on parade in the warm sunshine as the Victorian era gives way to the Edwardian. Note the children playing in the centre of the picture, and the sun awnings over the first-floor balconies. Victoria Parade stands on the East Cliff above Marine Road and the broad expanse of Ramsgate Sands.

RAMSGATE

VICTORIA PARADE 1901 / 48038

Part of the fleet of fishing smacks is seen in this unusual view of the harbour. Note the nets hung to dry in the foreground, while a dredger is moored in the centre of the picture.

RAMSGATE

THE HARBOUR 1907 / 58290

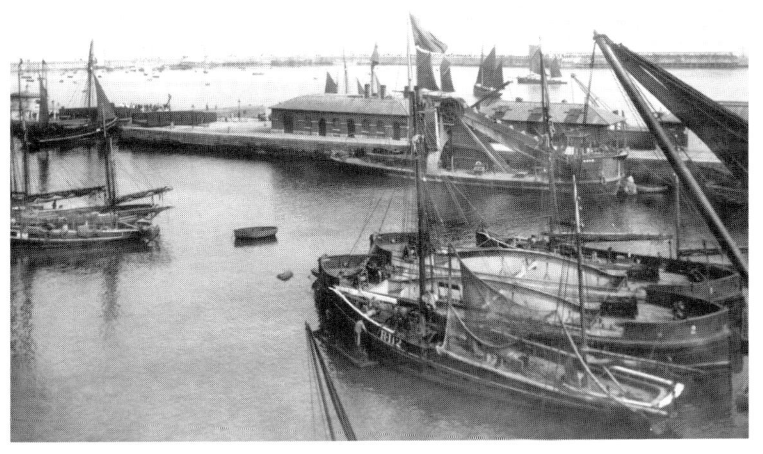

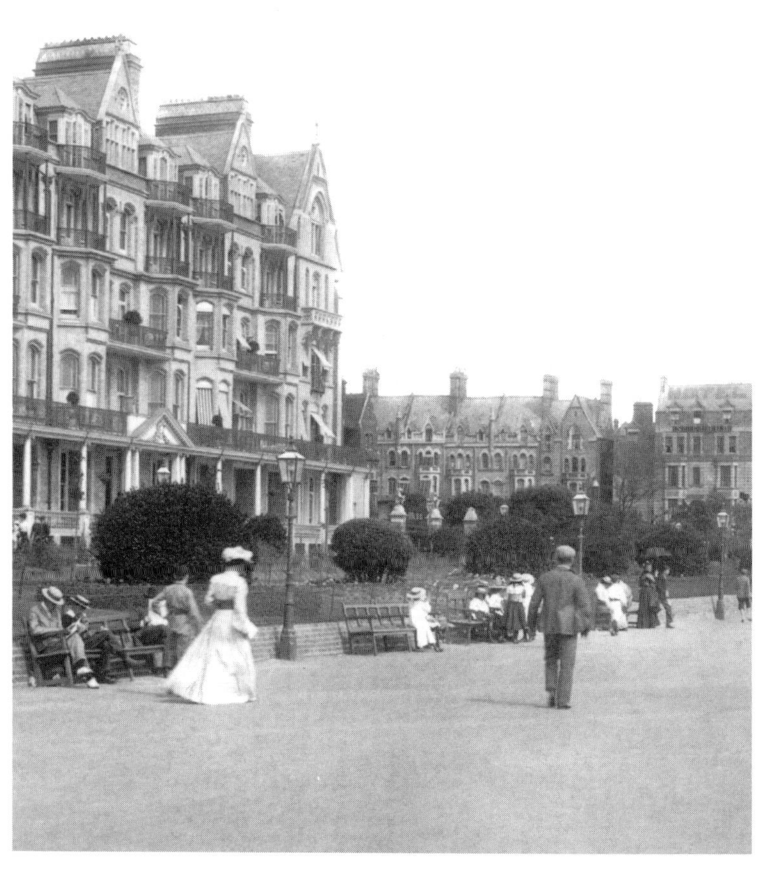

RAMSGATE

THE PROMENADE 1901 / 48039

This is virtually the same view as photograph number 48039, but taken some seventeen years later. The Granville Hotel seems little changed. Children with hoops pose for the photographer in the centre of the picture. The octagonal building on the left is a newspaper kiosk.

RAMSGATE

THE PROMENADE 1918 / 68463

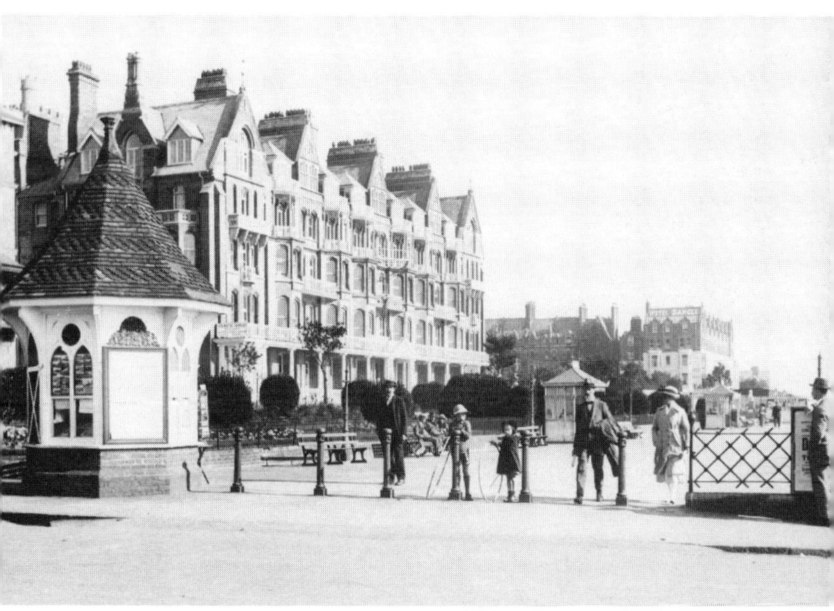

The Royal Victoria Pavilion, which stands close to the sands below the East Cliff, opened in 1904, and is pictured here when it was nearly new. It is now used as a casino, but in its heyday it was noted for its variety performances. Note the outer harbour cupped behind the massive east pier—the tip of the West Pier is just visible on the right.

RAMSGATE

THE PAVILION AND THE HARBOUR 1906 / 53466

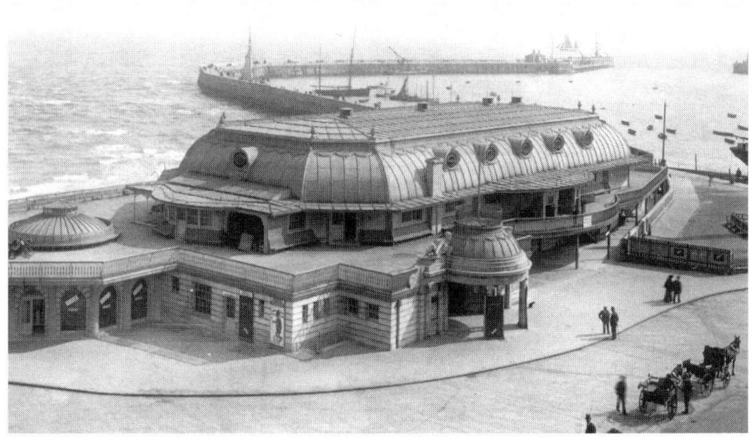

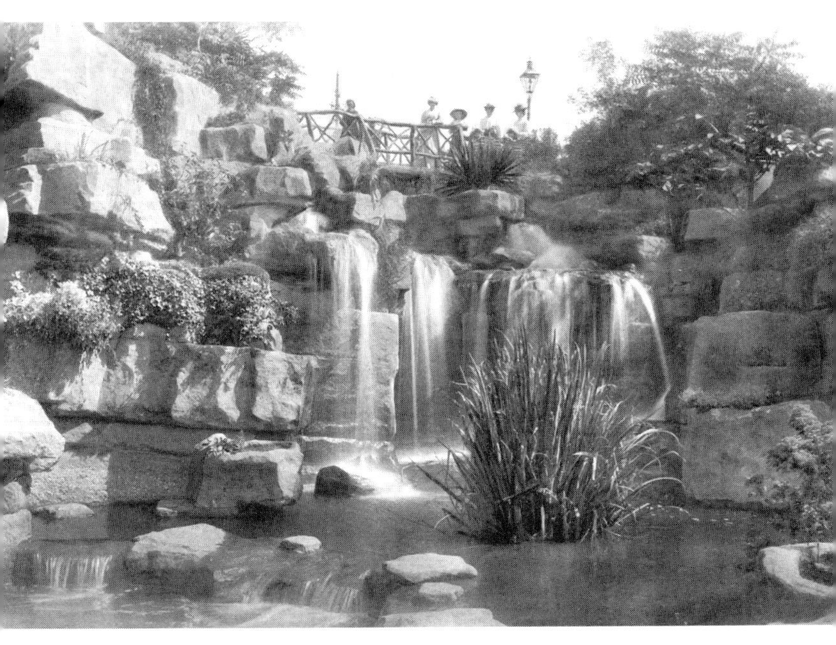

Passers-by on the rustic bridge, which was constructed at the same time as the ravine, pause to admire the waterfall which was part of the landscaping. This feature had become derelict, but has been renovated.

RAMSGATE

MADEIRA ROAD FOUNTAIN 1901 / 48043

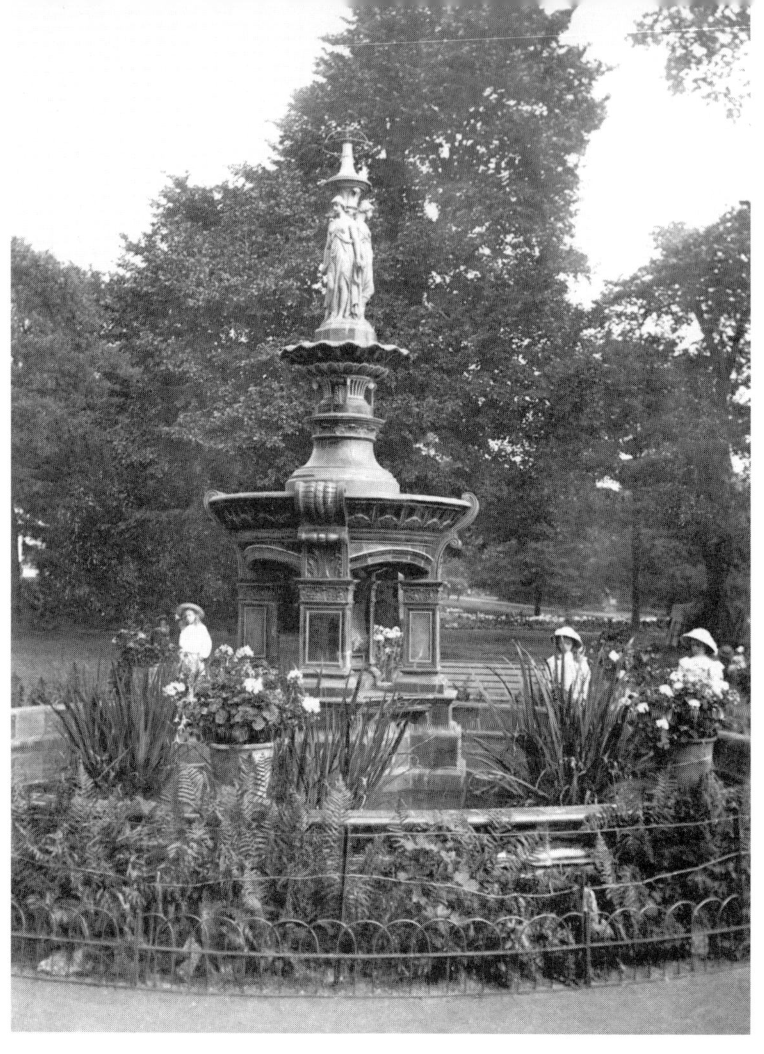

RAMSGATE

ELLINGTON GARDENS, THE PARK FOUNTAIN 1907 / 58282

Here we see the bandstand in Ellington gardens (now Ellington Park) a century ago: the magnificent trees and floral displays of this 12-acre open space are seen to advantage in this evocative picture.

RAMSGATE

ELLINGTON GARDENS 1901 / 48047

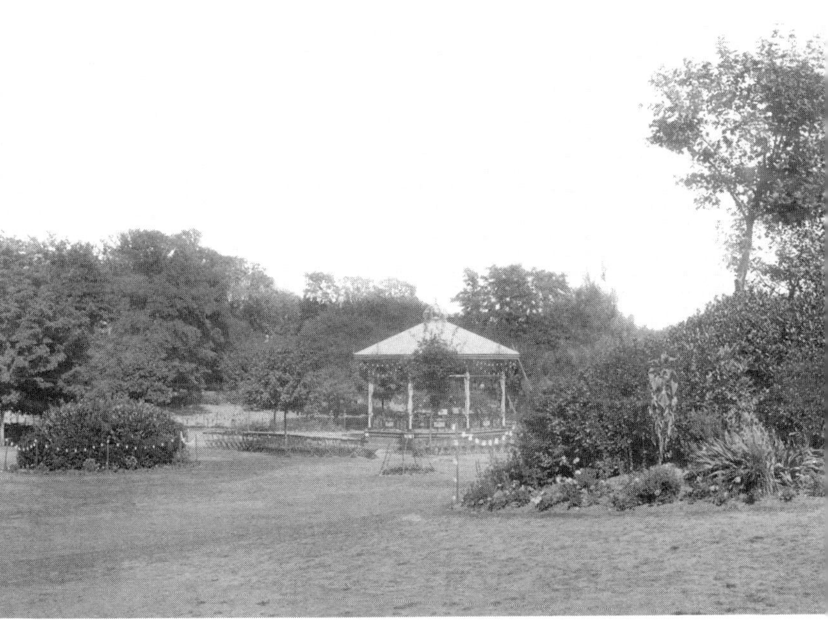

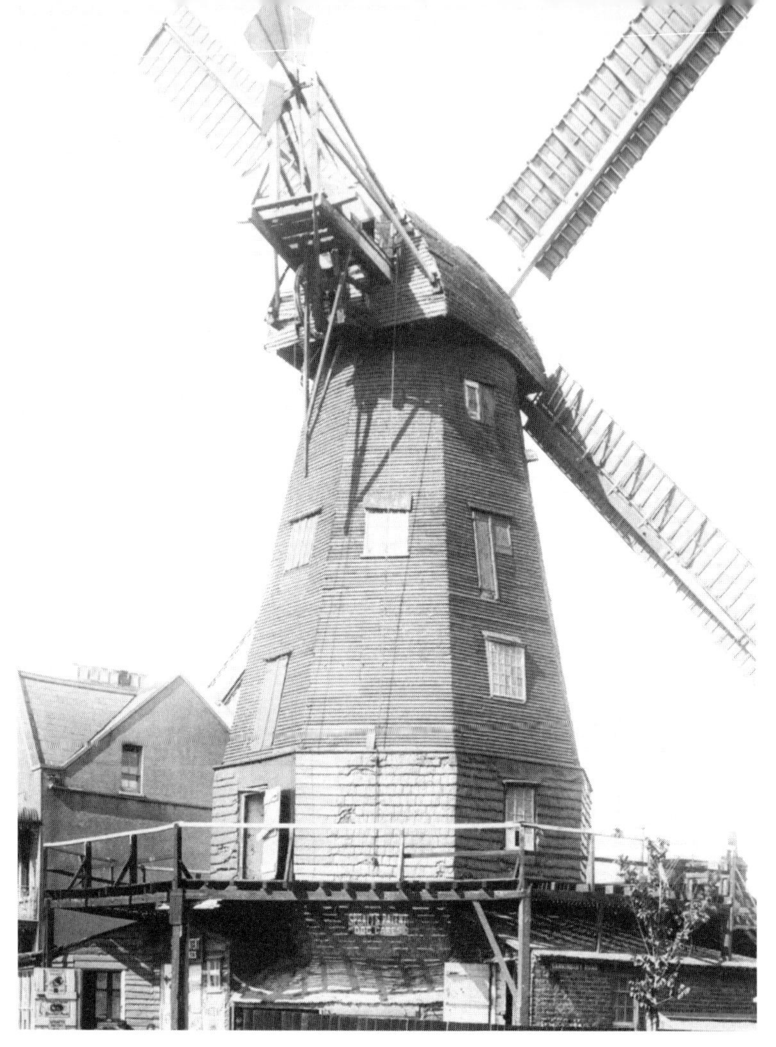

RAMSGATE

THE OLD MILL 1901 / 48045

The Bellevue Hotel at Pegwell is pictured here in its clifftop setting. The structure that is visible on the left was an artificial lagoon offering visitors sea-water bathing in safe, sheltered conditions. The former pier runs across the centre of the picture.

PEGWELL

THE SEA FRONT AND PIER c1880 / 12739

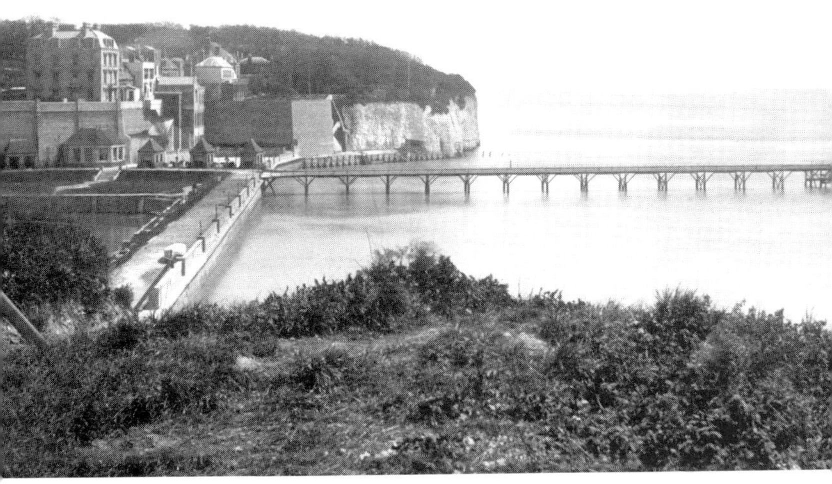

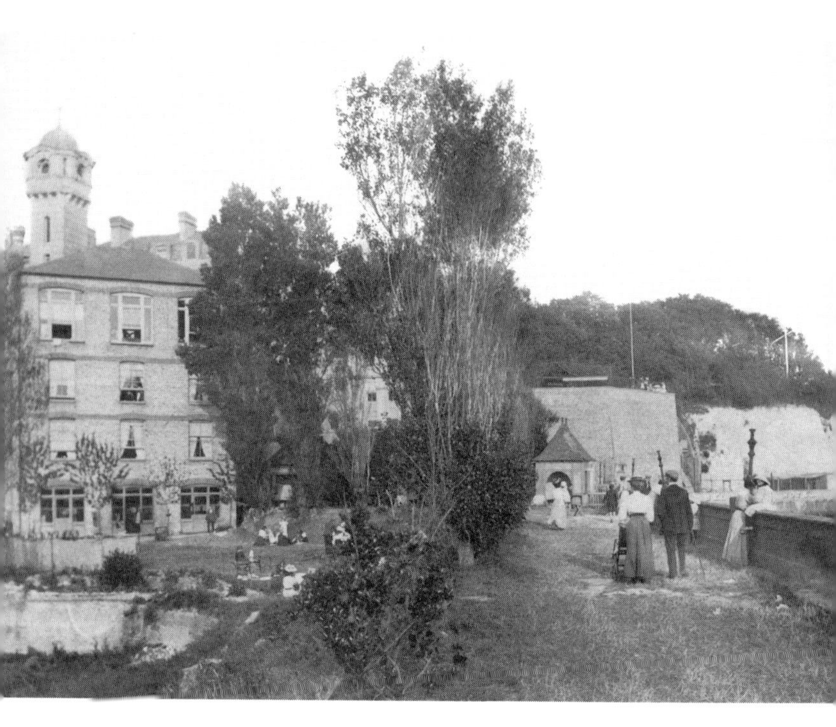

The coast has always been thought conducive to good health. Here inmates of Pegwell's Working Men's Convalescent Home stroll with their families. The home was noted for its sunken garden on reclaimed land, seen on the left below the sea wall.

PEGWELL

THE BAY 1907 / 58295

A further view of the Working Men's Convalescent Home, showing the sunken gardens, laid out on the dry bed of the former lagoon of the Belle Vue Hotel, which can be seen in the centre of the picture.

PEGWELL

THE CONVALESCENT HOME 1907 / 58298

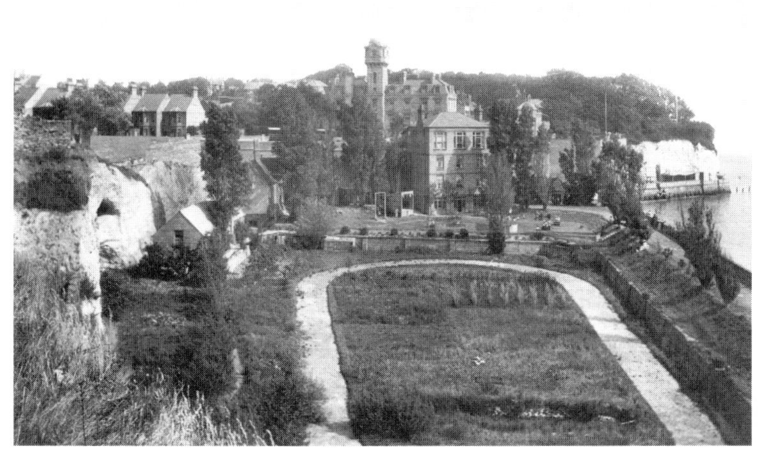

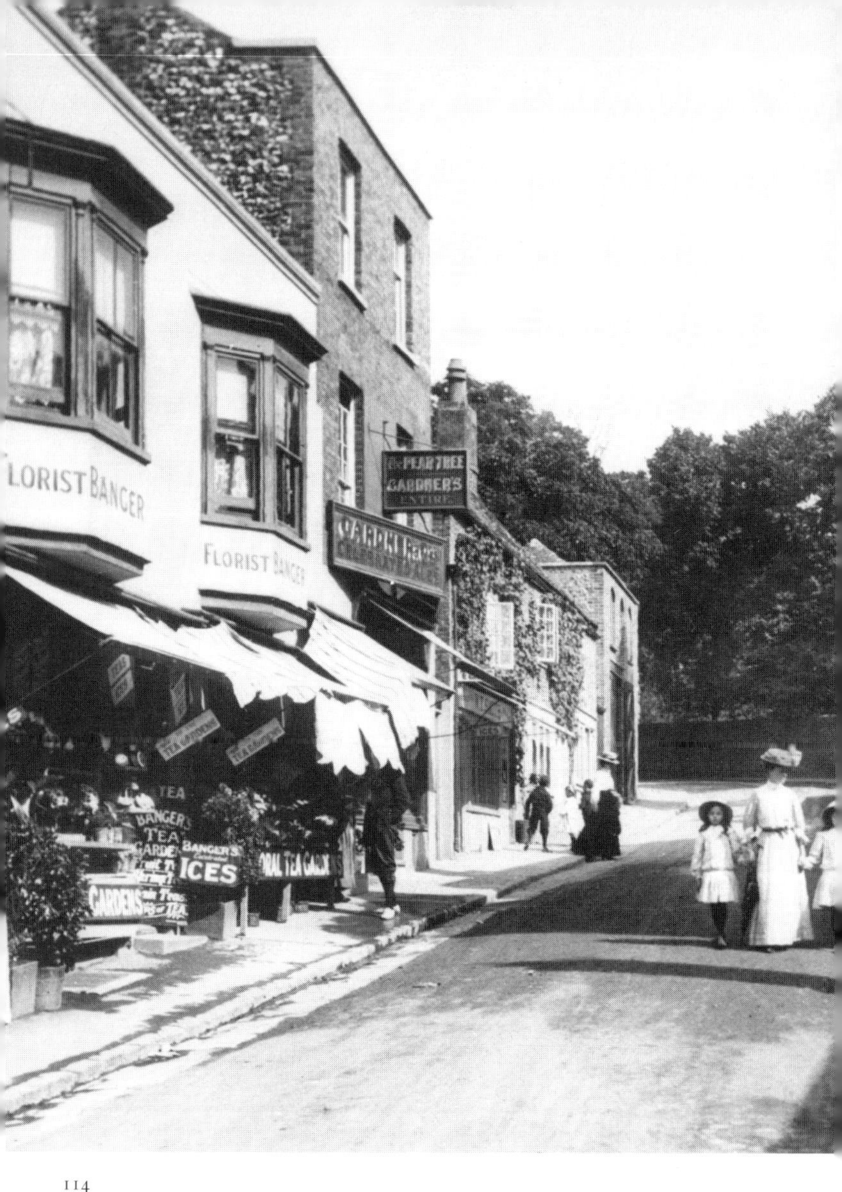
LORIST BANGER
FLORIST BANGER
PEAR TREE
GARDNERS
ENTIRE
TEA
BANGERS
TEA
BANGER'S
ICES
GARDENS

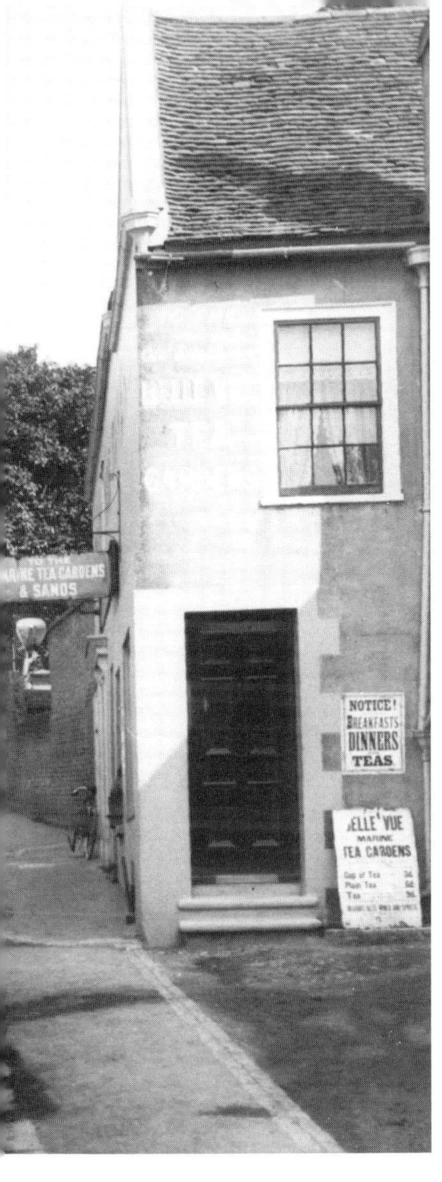

This prettily posed picture shows two little girls and a fashionable lady. The Belle Vue tea gardens, on the right, were built in 1790 and were very popular. They were visited in 1830 by the future Queen Victoria, who had tea there with her mother.

PEGWELL

THE VILLAGE 1907 / 58296

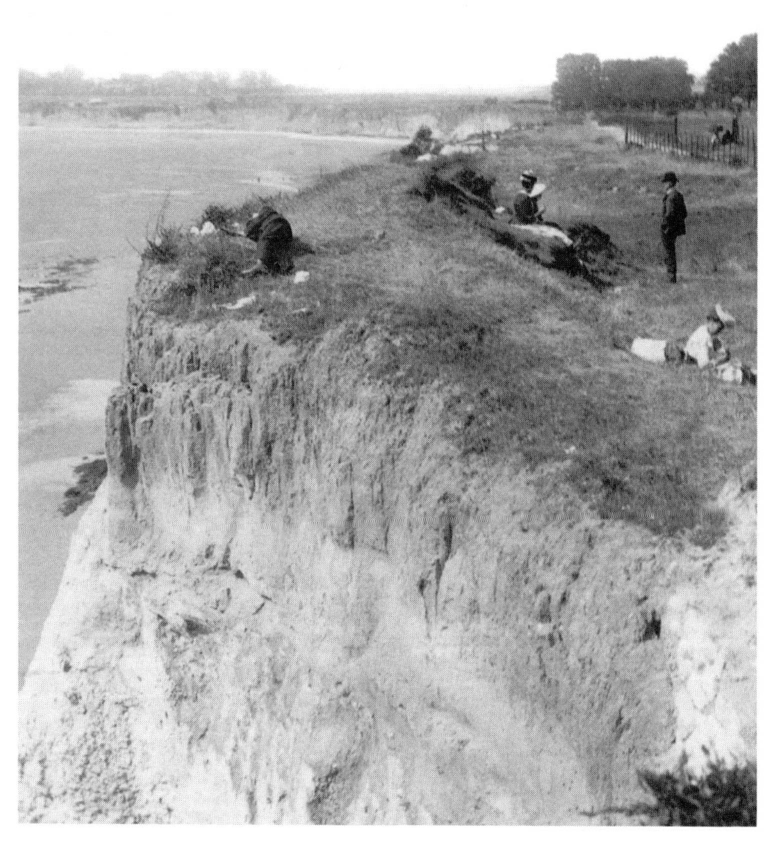

PEGWELL

THE BAY 1907 / 58302

Built in the 1840s, this row of coastguard cottages still stands, although Pegwell itself has been engulfed by Ramsgate. Smuggling was endemic in Thanet, and the Revenue was determined to stamp it out.

PEGWELL

COASTGUARD COTTAGES 1907 / 58306

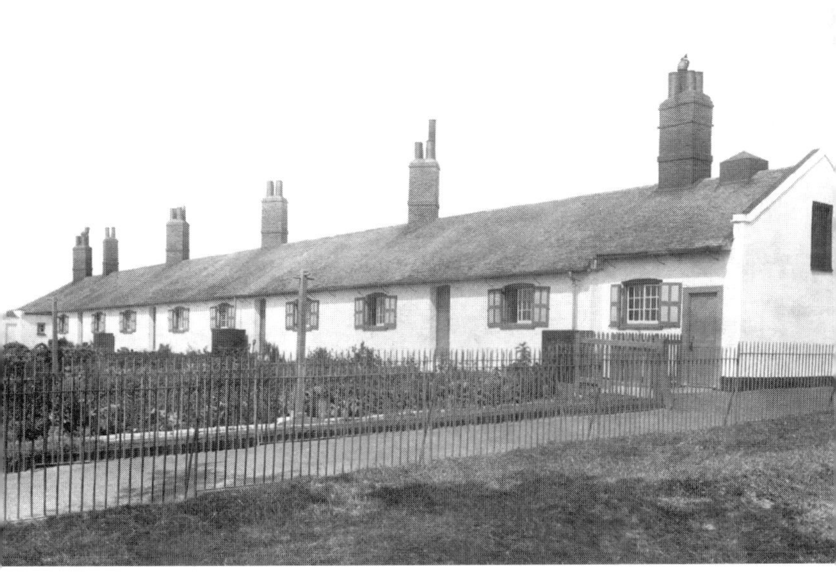

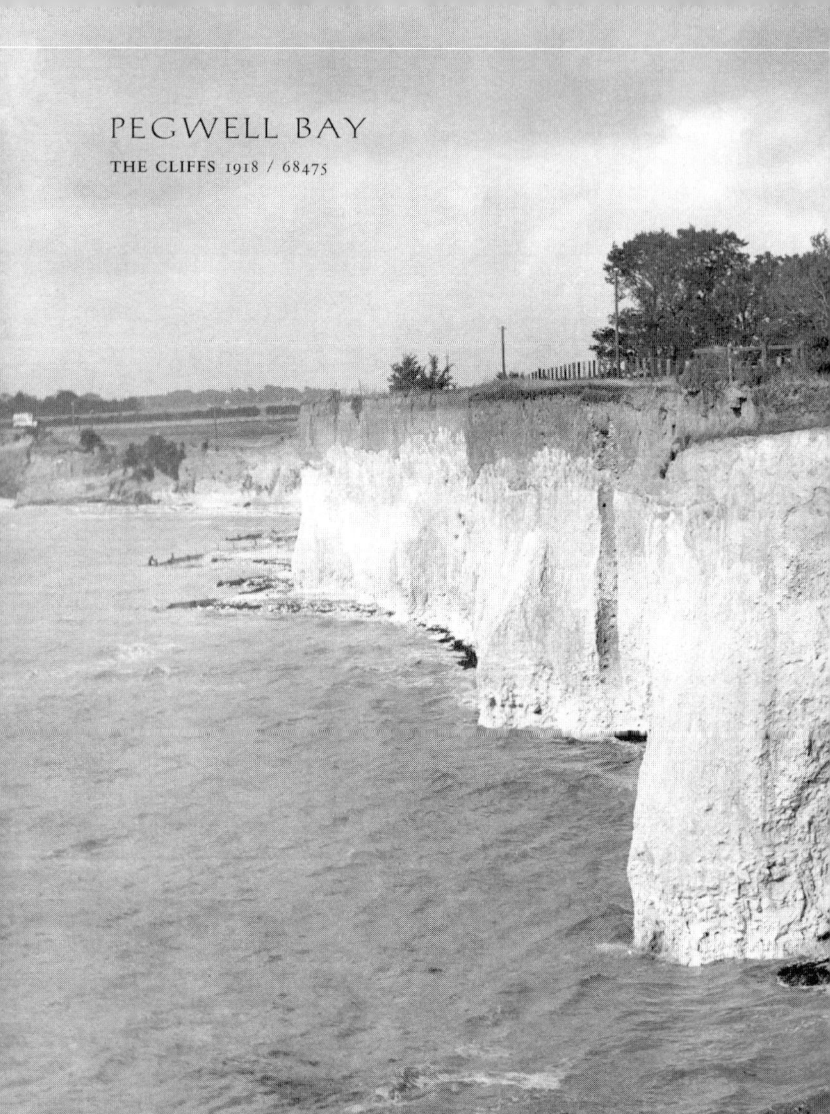

PEGWELL BAY

THE CLIFFS 1918 / 68475

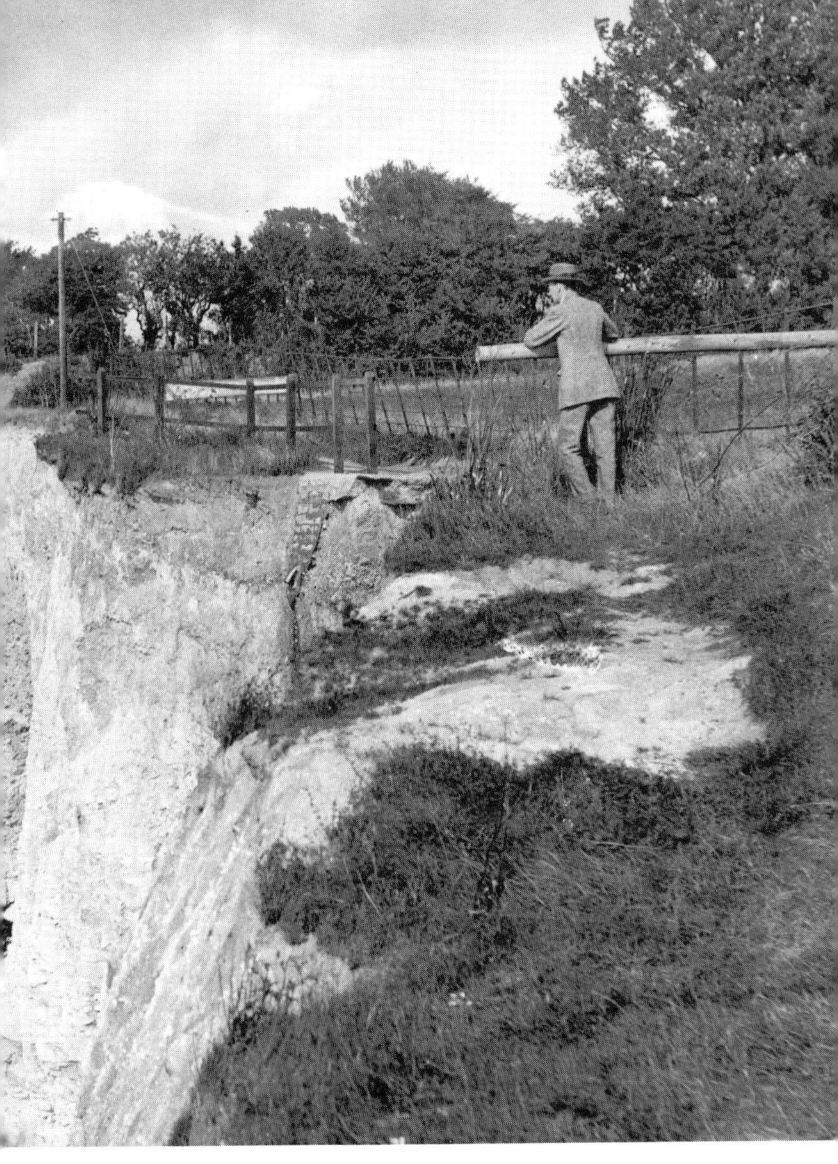

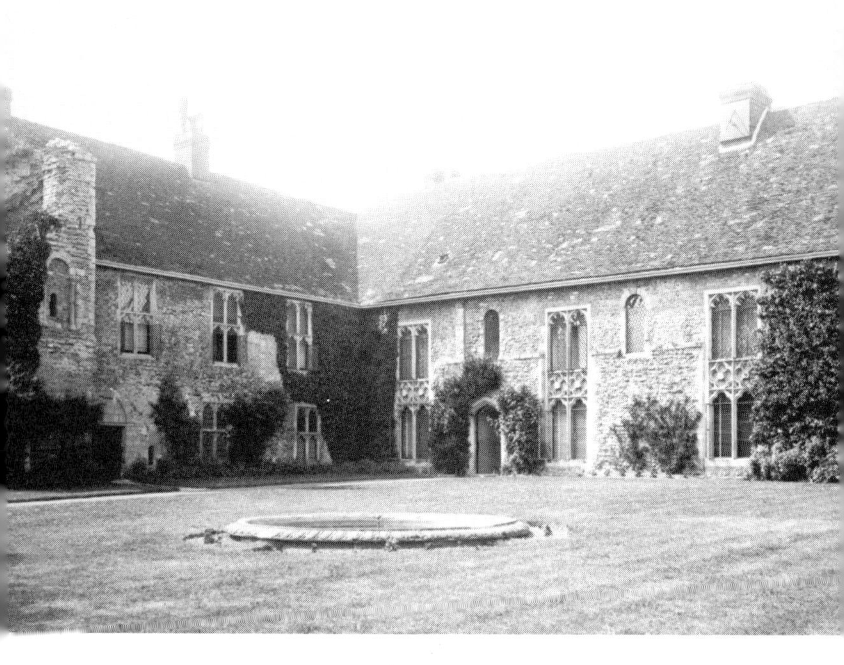

The original monastic settlement at Minster was founded in AD670, overlooking Minster Marshes, then the open Wantsum Channel. This late Victorian view shows the present buildings; they are of Norman age, built as a grange of St Augustine's Abbey in Canterbury. The buildings have been used as a nunnery since 1930.

MINSTER

MINSTER ABBEY 1894 / 34200

This peaceful view of Minster shows its pleasant old houses. Minster has the dubious claim to fame of being the site of the world's first fatal motor-car accident.

MINSTER

THE SQUARE c1955 / M86020

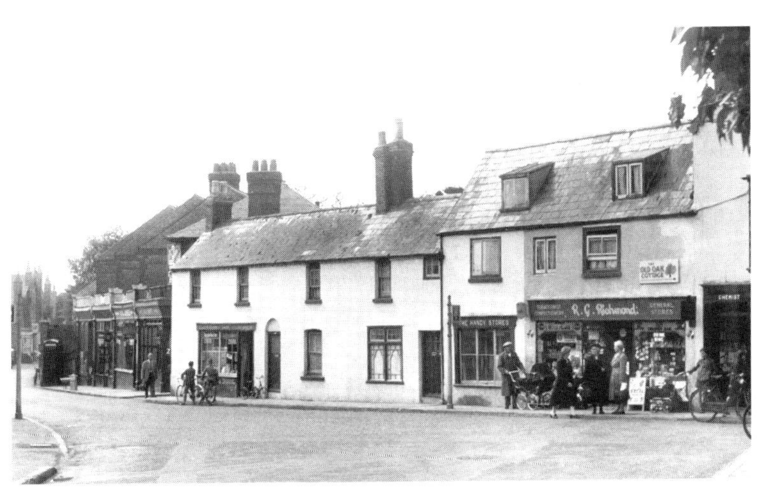

INDEX

PLEASE HELP US BRING FRITH'S PHOTOGRAPHS TO LIFE

Our authors do their best to recount the history of the places they write about. They give insights into how particular towns and villages developed, they describe the architecture of streets and buildings, and they discuss the lives of famous people who lived there. But however knowledgeable our authors are, the story they tell is necessarily incomplete.

Frith's photographs are so much more than plain historical documents. They are living proofs of the flow of human life down the generations. They show real people at real moments in history; and each of those people is the son or daughter of someone, the brother or sister, aunt or uncle, grandfather or grandmother of someone else. All of them lived, worked and played in the streets depicted in Frith's photographs.

We would be grateful if you would tell us about the many places shown in our photographs—the streets with their buildings, shops, businesses and industries. Describe your own memories of life in those streets: what it was like growing up there, who ran the local shop and what shopping was like years ago; if your workplace is shown tell us about your working day and what the building is used for now. With your help more and more Frith photographs can be brought to life, and vital memories preserved for posterity.

We will gradually add your comments and stories to the archive for the benefit of historians of the future. Wherever possible, we will try to include some of your comments in future editions of our books. Moreover, if you spot errors in dates, titles or other facts, please let us know, because our archive records are not always completely accurate—they rely on 150 years of human endeavour and hand-compiled records.

So please write, fax or email us with your stories and memories. Thank you!

CHOOSE ANY PHOTOGRAPH FROM THIS BOOK

for your FREE Mounted Print. Order further prints at half price

Fill in and cut out the voucher on the next page and return it with your remittance for £2.50 for postage, packing and handling to UK addresses (US $5.00 for USA and Canada). For all other overseas addresses include £5.00 post and handling. Choose any photograph included in this book. Make sure you quote its unique reference number eg. 42365 (it is mentioned after the photograph date. 1890 / 42365). Your SEPIA print will be approx 12" x 8" and mounted in a cream mount with a burgundy rule line (overall size 14" x 11").

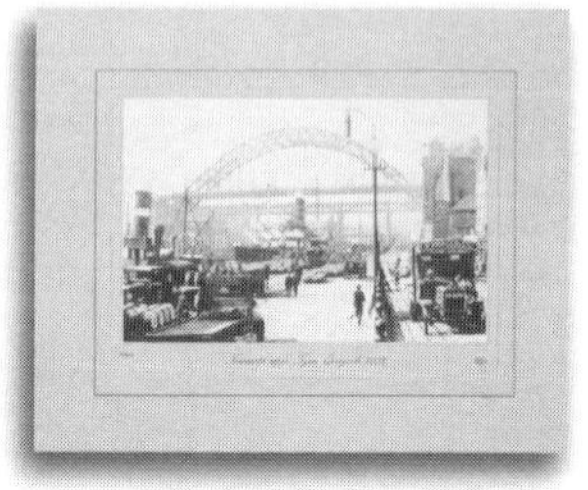

Mounted Print
Overall size 14 x 11 inches

Order additional Mounted Prints at HALF PRICE - If you would like to order more Frith prints from this book, possibly as gifts for friends and family, you can buy them at half price (with no extra postage and handling costs) - only £7.49 each (UK orders), US $14.99 each (USA and Canada).

*** IMPORTANT!**

These special prices are only available if you order at the same time as you order your free mounted print. You must use the ORIGINAL VOUCHER on the facing page (no copies permitted). We can only despatch to one address.

Have your Mounted Prints framed (UK orders only) - For an extra £14.95 per print you can have your mounted print(s) framed in an elegant polished wood and gilt moulding, overall size 16" x 13" (no additional postage).

FRITH PRODUCTS AND SERVICES

All Frith photographs are available for you to buy as framed or mounted prints. From time to time, other illustrated items such as Address Books, Calendars, Table Mats are also available. Already, almost 50,000 Frith archive photographs can be viewed and purchased on the internet through the Frith website.

For more detailed information on Frith companies and products, visit

www.francisfrith.co.uk

For further information, trade, or author enquiries, contact:

The Francis Frith Collection, Frith's Barn, Teffont, Salisbury SP3 5QP
Tel: +44 (0) 1722 716 376 Fax: +44 (0) 1722 716 881 Email: sales@francisfrith.co.uk

Voucher

for FREE and Reduced Price Frith Prints

Do not photocopy this voucher. Only the original is valid, so please fill it in, cut it out and return it to us with your order.

Picture ref no	Page number	Qty	Mounted @ £7.49 UK @$14.99 US	Framed + £14.95 (UK only)	US orders Total $	UK orders Total £
1		1	Free of charge*	£	$	£
2			£7.49 ($14.99)	£	$	£
3			£7.49 ($14.99)	£	$	£
4			£7.49 ($14.99)	£	$	£
5			£7.49 ($14.99)	£	$	£
6			£7.49 ($14.99)	£	$	£
Please allow 28 days for delivery			* Post & handling		$5.00	£2.50
			Total Order Cost US $			**£**

Title of this book ....

I enclose a cheque / postal order (UK) for £ .... $ ....
payable to 'Francis Frith Collection' (USA orders 'Frith USA Inc')

OR debit my Mastercard / Visa / Switch (UK) / Amex card / Discover (USA)
(credit cards only on non UK and US orders), card details below

Card Number

Issue No (Switch only) Valid from (Amex/Switch)

Expires Signature

Name Mr/Mrs/Ms ....

Address ....

....

....

Postcode/Zip.................................. Country ....

Daytime Tel No .... Valid to 31/12/06

PAYMENT CURRENCY: We only accept payment in £ Sterling or US $. If you are ordering **from any other country, please pay by credit card**, and you will be charged in one of these currencies.

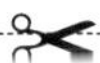

Send completed Voucher form to:

UK and rest of world - The Francis Frith Collection, Frith's Barn, Teffont, Salisbury, Wiltshire SP3 5QP England

USA and Canada orders - Frith USA Inc, 11447 Canterbury Lane, Parker, Colorado, 80138 USA

If you need more space, please write your address on a separate sheet of paper.